Educational Research Methods

J. D. Nisbet
*Professor of Education,*
*University of Aberdeen*

N. J. Entwistle
*Lecturer in Educational*
*Research,*
*University of Lancaster*

# Educational
# Research
# Methods

AMERICAN ELSEVIER PUBLISHING COMPANY, INC.
NEW YORK 1970

AMERICAN ELSEVIER PUBLISHING COMPANY, INC.
52 Vanderbilt Avenue, New York, N.Y. 10017

First printed 1970

Library of Congress Catalog Card Number: 79-114358
Standard Book Number: 444-19669-2

Printed and bound in Great Britain

# Contents

1. *Introduction*: Experiments and Surveys    7

2. Planning Research    16

3. Sampling    24

4. Interviews    32

5. Questionnaires    44

6. Data Processing    54

7. Environmental Factors    65

8. Abilities and Attainments    76

9. Examination Marks    92

10. Creativity and Divergent Thinking    106

11. Personality Assessment    114

12. Attitude Measurement    125

13. Observation and Case Studies    135

14. Curriculum Development    144

15. Interpreting Results    157

16. Writing the Report    167

    *Appendix:* Procedure for Research in Schools    177

    *References*    181

    *Acknowledgements*    187

    *Index*    188

## CHAPTER I

# Introduction:
# Experiments and Surveys

Too often the techniques and procedures of educational research are applied in a crude amateurish way. Many people have a rough idea of what is involved because they have themselves suffered as subjects of inquiry or have read of similar inquiries in books, magazine articles or even in advertisements. So they throw together a questionnaire or a check list or a scale, or devise a new form of test or conduct interviews, and produce the results as the evidence of research. It is not the purpose of this book to discourage the seeking of evidence to test our prejudices, but rather to call attention to the refinement of methods in educational research in recent years. As a result it is now possible to set down something like a standard form of procedure in a number of areas of educational research. These are mainly areas which involve quantitative or scientific methods of investigation. Of course, there are other important forms of research in education, such as historical or philosophical inquiry; and the researcher in these fields will find some material here which is relevant to his type of work also. A knowledge of the research methods described in this book is necessary for anyone who plans to embark on a research project, however elementary it may appear at first sight.

There is at present a serious shortage of persons trained and experienced in the relevant research methods. A newcomer to educational research, if he were to judge only from the choice of books currently available, might be excused for concluding that all he needs is a knowledge of statistics. There is no shortage of textbooks on statistics, elementary and advanced. Statistical techniques, however, represent only one aspect of research method, though it is an essential one. This book rarely mentions statistical procedures; it assumes that the reader either is familiar with statistics or has a good statistics textbook available. The emphasis throughout is on those techniques of measurement in which adequate published scales are *not* readily available. There are many books already available which describe published tests in detail. Where published tests are mentioned, it is usually so as to indicate the appropriate use of these tests in educational research. This emphasis may help to explain the way in which the various topics are treated.

The first three chapters deal with general aspects of design and planning of research. Chapter 3, which concerns sampling procedures, provides a link with the more general points which will be found in every elementary statistical text. Chapters 4 and 5 detail precisely the steps involved in conducting research interviews and using questionnaires correctly. Chapter 6 summarizes, in non-technical language, the wide range of methods of data processing available to suit the individual student working on a small scale and the professional team relying on computer facilities.

The next six chapters, 7 to 12, review techniques of measurement in three main areas, social, intellectual and attitudinal—how to develop and use assessments of environment or home background or social class, of abilities and attainment, and of personality and attitude. Two special lines of development, interaction analysis and curriculum study, are discussed in chapters 13 and 14; and the review concludes with chapters on pitfalls in interpreting results and guidance on report writing, together with an appendix on the appropriate procedure for research in schools.

SURVEYS

It is difficult to put research into neat categories: many research projects involve a variety of approaches. A general distinction may be drawn between surveys, or descriptive research, and experimental studies. The term 'survey' is used here for the wide range of studies which involve observation of a situation as it is, without setting up experimental conditions or allocating groups to different treatments. But surveys are more than the mere recording of information—how much pocket money, what hour of bed-time, what percentage favour corporal punishment? Surveys may include the use of tests, examining the distribution of scores or the application of sophisticated techniques of measurement to contrasting groups which already exist within the educational system. By the design of the survey, and in particular by the choice of samples, one introduces an element of the experimental into the survey. An imaginative use of survey methods may provide evidence on questions which cannot be treated by experimental procedures on children: for example, the use of an existing situation which incorporates the equivalent of an experimental design, as in studies of deaf children, or bi-linguals, to investigate the process of language development.

The element of comparison almost inevitably enters into survey work, if it is to be of value; either comparison with the over-all scores of a large sample, or surveys of two groups which allow comparisons. The performance of rural children and urban children on a verbal reasoning test with a strict time-limit offers one such comparison. Similarly a survey might contrast differences between parents and teachers in their attitudes to parent–teacher organizations. Even general surveys may provide a basis for comparison when the data can be sub-divided into categories. A classic example is the survey of early leaving from secondary schools (Ministry of Education, 1954), * in which the data were sub-divided by ability level and by social class. Tables showed the proportions of able children who abandoned their secondary school courses, and the differences in these proportions for different social classes.

One of the earliest objective investigations in education was a survey of the 'spelling grind' by Rice, in 1897. He collected information on the average time per day spent in learning spelling in American elementary schools, and also on the standard of spelling in each of the schools visited; there was, surprisingly,

*All the references are given on p. 181ff.

no relation between attainment in spelling and time spent. Survey research has developed in sophistication and in scale since then. At the opposite extreme to Rice's pioneer study, there are the Scottish Mental Surveys of 1936 and 1947, in which the entire eleven-year-old population of Scotland in each of these years was given the same test, and the results were used as a check on the theory that differential fertility—the higher birth-rate among less intelligent people—was likely to produce a decline in the level of national intelligence (Scottish Council for Research in Education, 1949). Every four years from 1948 to 1964, national reading surveys have been conducted in England, using carefully selected samples as a check on reading standards in the nation (Department of Education and Science, 1966). The survey work for the Plowden Report (Department of Education and Science, 1967) is presented in great detail. Volume 2, which contains these results, is as large as volume 1, which contains the Report itself.

These examples indicate the range in subject matter and complexity covered by the survey approach to educational research. The value of this approach depends largely on how representative is the sample chosen for the survey. Small-scale studies restricted to one area or one school may give information of value to the specific group concerned, but the results may conflict with those from parallel studies of other groups. The question of how to choose an appropriate sample is therefore of crucial importance. This topic is developed in chapter 3.

A serious limitation in the survey approach is the lack of evidence about causality in the relations detected. We may find that there is a correlation between colour preference and school attainment. Those children who choose garish colours tend to do badly in exams. But we cannot suggest that colour preference *causes* the poor exam performance. The correlation establishes only concomitant variation; certain values in one measure tend to be associated with particular values in another measure. It is not possible to *prove* causality, but where one event is invariably *followed* by another, a causal link may be inferred. In surveys it is usual to collect all the information at the same point in time, preventing any knowledge of which events occur first. Even in a follow-up study in which information is collected over a period of years only a limited amount of evidence of causality may be found. So often in a social situation many of the variables are interrelated. The survey method contributes little to our understanding of which of the underlying factors are influential, unless a complex statistical analysis is undertaken. Simple statistics can in fact be misleading. The highest correlation or most significant value of a chi-square test does not point necessarily to the main factor. These results may show only that certain measures are the most reliable, while the important factors have been measured too crudely. Indeed, the most important factor may have been omitted from the investigation altogether.

These warnings are not intended to imply that the survey method is inappropriate in educational research: this method is used (and misused) more widely than experimental techniques. Great caution must, however, be taken in interpreting the results of surveys and, in particular, when attempting to infer causality.

## EXPERIMENTAL DESIGNS

The difficulties met in using the survey approach are less severe in an experimental design, but other types of difficulty appear. In the simplest form of experimental design, a change is made in the value of one variable—the *independent variable*—and the effect of this change on another variable is observed—the *dependent variable*. Rice's survey of spelling was described above. An experimental version of this study might compare the progress in spelling made by two groups of children. One group continues spending the same time on spelling as before. This group—the *control group*—is used as a standard against which to compare the effect of changes in the independent variable (time spent on spelling). The other group—the *experimental group*—is given less time on spelling, and the performance of these children in a later test of spelling is compared with that of the control group. Again one cannot be sure that one change has *caused* the other: less time on spelling may mean more time on reading, or more attention during the spelling lesson. The teacher may develop a more favourable attitude towards teaching as a result of the interest of the research worker (Hawthorne effect) and this may be the real cause of changes in the children's performance.

The influence of other factors can be controlled to some extent. The attempt to control or randomize all variables except those being investigated is central to the experimental method. A variable may be *randomized* by increasing the scale of the study. If type of school or age of teacher is suspected to be influential, a large sample containing all the different types of school and a complete range of ages among teachers might be used. As no one type of school or age of teacher predominates, their effects cancel each other out and cannot affect the result of the experiment. If a smaller study is being used, these variables may be *controlled* by careful choice of schools and teachers being used and by making sure that the influence of these variables is eliminated.

Even where the effect of extraneous variables has been controlled or randomized, it is still crucial to ensure that the experimental groups and control groups are equivalent. Only then can a change in performance in spelling be attributed to the change in teaching method. Again the groups can be made equivalent by *matching* or by *random allocation*. In the latter method all pupils in the schools involved would be given a number and a table of random numbers would be used to place pupils in the two groups. Alternatively, names might be drawn out of a hat. If the groups are large enough, the chances of the groups differing in any important way become small. The alternative approach— matching—attempts to identify the important variables which might affect performance and to ensure that the groups are equal in terms of these variables. Each member of the experimental group is matched with a member of the control group who has the same attributes—say sex, age, social class, intelligence and spelling ability. To form the groups, it is necessary to have measures of all the variables considered important and to identify pupils having as nearly as possible the same patterns of scores. Pairs of comparable children are then allocated randomly (by tossing a coin, say) into experimental and control groups.

Splitting up comparable pairs is the surest way of forming comparable groups, but it is not always practicable. If this method is not possible, a modified form of grouping may be used in which pupils are chosen so that the over-all distributions of scores or characteristics of the *groups as a whole* are equal. It is much easier to form groups which are equivalent as a whole than to find exactly comparable pairs of children.

Besides being comparable, the groups must remain representative of all the pupils originally considered before matching. In forming groups many of the children may be left out altogether. Pupils for whom no matching partners have been found may have to be excluded. If the groups are no longer representative, the results cannot be generalized. The whole problem of choosing representative samples and the dangers in using biased samples is discussed later.

The remaining part of the simple experiment on spelling might continue as follows. Control and experimental groups comparable in sex, age, social class, intelligence and spelling ability would be obtained and the two groups given the *pre-test*. The test is designed to measure the dependent variable and in this example would be a spelling test covering not only words previously learned but also the new words to be introduced during the experimental period. The control group would continue being taught as before; thus the independent variable would be kept constant. The experimental group would be taught for a shorter period, thereby introducing the required change. After the duration of the experiment both groups would be given the *post-test,* either the same spelling test or a parallel version of it. The performance of the two groups would be compared and the significance of the difference between the mean scores would be tested statistically.

This is an over-simplified example. It might well be that there is an optimum period for a spelling lesson. The comparison between two groups would give no evidence of this. However, if several experimental groups taught for differing lengths of time were used as well as a control group which was not taught spelling at all, the comparison of the series of mean scores might well show evidence of an optimum length of instruction. The statistical method devised to deal with two or more equivalent groups is the analysis of variance. Simple two-way analysis of variance enables us to deal with the above problem which contains two variables (spelling performance against period of instruction), but since educational problems usually involve many variables, the experimental design may have to be more complex. Controlling variables has one severe disadvantage. We cannot then find how these variables might themselves affect the experiment. Clearly intelligence will influence spelling proficiency; there might also be sex differences. A complex experimental design would allow the separate effects of several independent variables to be investigated (spelling performance against period of instruction × intelligence × sex). There may also be interactions between these: a period of instruction of one length may be more effective with the brighter girls and the duller boys, while another length may be more effective with the duller girls and brighter boys. Interaction effects as identified by analysis of variance may be quite complex. For example, a period of instruction of one length may prove more effective when one method is adopted, but a different length of period is more appropriate to another method (period × method interaction). Or a certain length of period proves best for, say, younger boys and older girls, and a different length for older boys and younger girls (period × sex × age interaction).

The statistical technique of analysis of variance is still appropriate for these complex experimental designs; the reader is referred to one of the many texts available—for example, Lewis' (1968) *Experimental Design in Education*. Another example of a study using an experimental design will be discussed in chapter 14. Curriculum development is an area where carefully designed experimental studies might make an important contribution to educational research. This brief discussion of the two broad approaches to educational research—survey and experimental—shows something of their characteristic strengths and weaknesses, but this division cannot be thought of as a clear-cut distinction. It is sometimes difficult to be sure which method has been adopted. Nor do all research studies fit into these categories. No mention has been made of the clinical or *case study* method in which small groups or individual children are observed or tested in great detail, often as a preliminary to larger-scale study. Some typical methods of measurement used in detailed observations of this type are discussed in chapter 13. But whatever pattern of research is adopted, careful planning is an essential first step. Both experimental and survey methods are systematic scientific attempts at understanding educational problems, and these demand considerable forethought before any information is collected. The procedure for planning a research project is the topic of chapter 2.

## SUMMARY

Most educational research studies are planned as either *surveys* or *experiments*. Surveys are used to describe existing situations; the variables are measured within the normal educational setting. Careful selection of the sample is essential, but even with a representative group causality cannot be proved, thought it may be inferred where one event is invariably followed by another. Surveys enable us to measure the relations between important educational and social variables in a realistic setting. With care it is possible to choose sub-samples—for example, deaf children and pupils with unimpaired hearing—so as to introduce into surveys an element of the experimental method.

In an experiment, the value of the independent variable is manipulated so as to introduce differences between the control group and the experimental groups. All these groups must be made equivalent either by matching or by random allocation, while remaining representative. The usual approach is to detect changes in the dependent variable by use of a pre-test and a post-test. Differences between groups in scores on the post-test are then compared using an analysis of variance technique.

CHAPTER 2 | Planning Research

The stereotype of the research worker as a 'back-room boy', working on his own and somewhat isolated from reality, is misleading if it is applied to research in education. Team work, practical experience, close collaboration with teachers and other professional workers in education, an understanding of children— all of these are more likely to be characteristic of research in education nowadays. But there is a grain of truth in the old-fashioned stereotype, in that research is essentially a strategy of thinking and not merely a programme for action. The techniques of research described in this book provide means which help to sharpen thinking about educational problems. The raw material of research is not pieces of information, but ideas—ideas which are tested and modified by the collection of evidence so as either to confirm their validity or to show up their inadequacy.

The work involved in a research project can be divided into seven stages:

1. Identifying and precisely defining the problem.
2. Reading previous research on relevant topics.
3. Deciding on techniques to be used for collecting and analysing information.
4. Selecting and defining the sample to be studied.
5. Collecting the data.
6. Processing, analysing and interpreting the results.
7. Writing up the report.

DEFINING THE PROBLEM

Stages 1 and 2 go together. These initial stages are the most important in the whole process, for the value of all the rest depends on how thoroughly the problem has been thought out at the start. Ideas take shape against the background of one's knowledge: the more extensive this knowledge the more likely the ideas will be of value. Knowledge of the social sciences, of psychology and sociology, is necessary to provide the general theoretical concepts which we must use in thinking about problems of learning or behaviour. Knowledge of children and personal observation of their ways of thinking and behaving is also important, together with knowledge of the actual conditions in schools. Ideas for research have to be original, but they are most effectively developed out of a study of what other research workers have written. Starting with a general idea, you must read as widely as possible to discover how others have tackled this problem. As you read, you formulate specific questions or tentative hypotheses, which define the area of your problem more precisely. The reading should not be too narrowly restricted to the topic of interest: important contributions to research result from 'cross-fertilization'—the application of a technique or approach from one area of research to a problem in another area, where its application had not previously been considered. Further reading brings the general research topic into sharper focus, and shows how it may best be examined. The topic or idea must now be framed in a way that makes it accessible, and here you must take account of the availability of relevant information. Almost invariably this leads to a narrowing of the scope of inquiry by selecting this or that aspect as having priority. A conclusive finding on a relatively restricted aspect of a problem is of more value than an investigation which fails to reach a firm conclusion because it tries to cover too much.

A useful way of recording the review material is to write out small cards for each book or article read. The card carries the author's name, the date of publication, the title and either the publisher or details of the journal. An example of a typical lay-out is shown in figure 1, p. 18.

The two initial stages in the work are perhaps the most difficult of all. They are certainly the ones which cause the researcher the greatest stress. The capacity to tolerate stress of this kind is an

FINGER, J. A. and SCHLESSER, G. E. (1965) *School Review*, **73**, 14–29
'Non-intellective predictors of academic success in school and college.'
*Notes* Reports a factor analysis of the Personal Values Inventory which produces a factor of 'academic achievement motivation'. This factor contributes to the prediction of academic success with as much weight as an aptitude test.
*Sample* 1,000+ pupils and students in American colleges and high schools (ages 14–19).
*Cross-references* Schlesser, G. E. and Finger, J. A. (1962); Austin, H. R. (1965)

Figure 1. Card index for review article

essential quality of mind in research. A student who has only a limited time in which to complete a project is inclined to rush into a decision on his topic of inquiry before he has thought out what it involves, and before he has discovered the obstacles and the ways of overcoming them which previous workers in this field have reported. It is quite possible after a month of reading and reflection for him to remain undecided about how to proceed, and to feel despair at his lack of progress.

A less common fault at the opposite extreme is to spend time obsessionally in reading and planning so that there is no time left for carrying out the project adequately and for writing up the results. Commonly, a student's reaction as he begins to find his way among the research literature in a field of inquiry is dismay and discouragement—or even panic: either nothing seems relevant, or every possibility has already been covered. Even if a worth-while topic has been decided, it is unnerving to find additional references at the end of each article which provide a further reading list. At first, the number of papers to be consulted increases with alarming rapidity; but soon he finds familiar titles recurring, and ideally he should reach a stage where no new papers of any value appear among the references. He then has 'mastered the literature'.

However, this is an ideal situation which is seldom reached. Most of us have to work to a time-limit, whether we are students preparing a thesis for a predetermined date of submission or a full-time professional team working to a programme determined by the finance budget. In these circumstances, an appropriate division of time is to allot one third to planning (stages 1 to 4), one third to the collection and analysis of data (stages 5 and 6), and one third to the writing of the report (stage 7). Too often, the inexperienced research worker rushes ahead to stage 5, seeking the reassurance of collecting data, of having something to show; and he fails to leave enough time for the unexpected demands of stage 7, the writing up of results. Planning obviously requires time, because no amount of sophisticated statistical analysis can derive worth-while results from a badly designed inquiry. There is something of a paradox in that the planning of a research project is unlikely to be successful unless we have some ideas of the results we are likely to find. This does not mean that we can only investigate problems where the answers are known beforehand. It means that, in the initial stages, thinking must be in terms of hypotheses or specific questions which we think might be answered by analysing the information collected during our inquiries.

MEASUREMENT AND SAMPLING

Stages 3 and 4 deal with decisions on techniques of measurement and analysis, and the choice of sample. In these stages, the planning of the project becomes more precise. The time, money and help available are factors which will determine the scale of the research: it is important to tackle a problem on a large enough scale to give worth-while results, and yet realistically taking account of what can be covered with the facilities to hand. Choice of techniques and sampling are interrelated, since, given limited facilities, elaborate or time-consuming methods of obtaining information usually lead to a restriction in sample size: with simple procedures, large numbers can be covered. (This applies not only to statistical inquiries: in a historical study, for example, the more detailed the analysis the smaller is the coverage.) Nevertheless, a start must be made somewhere and it is usual for a provisional decision on techniques to precede a decision on sampling. For example, some techniques in educational research can only be applied individually or by an experienced tester. Certain methods of statistical analysis impose very strict limitations on procedure for selecting the sample from whom the information is to be obtained. The problem of determining the appropriate size of sample, large enough to give significant results but still economical in use of resources, is dealt with in chapter 3.

Perhaps this account of the early stages of a research inquiry sounds too elaborate. Certainly one should not be too closely bound to a rigid procedure. The experienced research worker does not distinguish these four stages in his mind as he moves through the planning stage. Inevitably there is an interaction between many considerations: the complexity of the problem, how far the topic has been adequately developed by previous research, the number of variables included and the nature of the relations being studied. Thus, in a study of sharply contrasting variables using clear-cut techniques, it may be possible to limit sample size. On the other hand, in studies in which weak or indirect relations are expected or in which a large number of variables is included, much larger samples may be required. If the analysis demands the use of an intricate statistical procedure or a division into sub-groups, again a large sample may be necessary.

These guide-lines for devising the research design over-simplify this difficult problem. You may catch a sunbeam more readily than write down clear-cut rules for planning a sound original research project. But one general rule can be stated simply: allow sufficient time for these difficult and uncomfortable planning stages.

## COLLECTING, PROCESSING AND ANALYSING DATA

With stage 5, collecting the data, a research student may feel that at last he has started on the work proper. In stage 6—data processing, statistical analysis and interpretation—he may see himself as using those specialized skills which he has mastered with such difficulty. Most textbooks on educational research concentrate on one aspect—statistical analysis—so exclusively as to suggest that there is nothing else of importance in research. An understanding of statistical methods certainly is essential, but any detailed treatment of statistical procedures is beyond the scope of this book. Some simple statistical concepts are introduced in the next chapter, while chapter 15 deals with problems of interpretation, which are often neglected in courses on statistics.

Precise application of research techniques, accurate sampling, meticulous recording, checking the marking of tests to eliminate errors (the error rate should be below 1 item in 10,000)—all these are distinguishing features of a good research worker. Yet these two stages, 5 and 6, are the ones which can most readily be handed over to the research assistant, the clerical worker and computer operator. It is the other stages which demand the greatest skill and experience. In our allocation of time in a research project, we suggested one third for planning and not more than one third for stages 5 and 6, that is, for carrying out the plan. The remaining one third is left for writing the report.

WRITING THE REPORT

This final stage in the research project is discussed more fully in chapter 16. Here we simply stress the importance of treating this final stage with particular care, as it demands thought, attention and time. At present this is the aspect of research which is worst done, and yet it is important. Careful communication of research is almost as important as its execution. A lucid, carefully argued research report is difficult to write and it also takes time. Technical aspects in particular take longer than one normally expects—designing the lay-out of tables, checking figures, compiling and checking references for the bibliography. Time must also be left for further analysis of the results to check unexpected findings or to follow up additional leads suggested in the main analysis. The experienced research worker writes up a draft of his material as he proceeds. But knowing how often some unexpected disaster upsets the best of plans, he is wise if he leaves himself (and the typist) a fair margin of time at the end.

Educational research is not just experiment or collecting information: it is a way of thinking about education. Innovation is often glibly justified in terms of 'research'. Without evaluation by an adequately designed programme of inquiry, mere innovation will tell us little. It is equally useless to collect data and then see what you can make of it; information in itself is of little value. For example, an experiment which shows that the use of i.t.a. produces better results than traditional methods of teaching reading is open to a variety of explanations, as we shall see in chapter 14; it does not justify a wholesale abandonment of the traditional in favour of the novel. In the 1950s, a survey revealed that children in Scotland went to the cinema more frequently than children in England, and that children in the north of England went more frequently than children in the south of England. Without a theoretical basis to this survey, the information by itself is useless, except perhaps to cinema managers. The researcher who asks several teachers to mark the same set of essays must have some strategy of analysis and experiment in mind. If their marks fail to show close agreement, how can this be explained? What will the next step be? How can one check on this explanation? It is necessary throughout to work by the light of some general idea or hypothesis. This idea gives unity to the whole investigation, to the analysis of results, and to the writing up of the report. Experimentation is not a way of avoiding thinking. Much educational research is useless because it lacks critical thinking at each stage.

SUMMARY

Knowledge about the techniques of research—the main topic of this book—is not enough in itself. This knowledge must be related to knowledge of basic social sciences, knowledge of statistical procedures and knowledge of schools and of children. In research the first stages—the planning stages—are the hardest and the most crucial.

1. Identify and define the problem.
2. Read relevant previous work.
3. Decide on appropriate techniques.
4. Select and define the sample.

Throughout these stages, the strategy is to design a situation which will produce relevant evidence to prove or disprove a hypothesis or give answers to a specific question. These four stages require at least one third of the time available for the whole project.

5. Collect the data.
6. Process, analyse and interpret the results.

These two stages should not be allowed to take up more than one third of the time.

7. Write the report.

This final stage will require all the time there is left.

## CHAPTER 3

Sampling

It is often difficult for students meeting the techniques of educational research for the first time to appreciate why tests of statistical significance need to be applied at all. If, in an experiment, the experimental group improves while the control group does not improve, why is there still argument as to whether there is any 'real' difference? If, in a survey, women students are found to spend longer studying than men, surely that is the answer. The need for tests of statistical significance is appreciated only when it is realized that the research worker is interested in generalizing his results. He is not just interested in the students he has chosen for his survey: he is interested in students or a certain category of students in general. He hopes to demonstrate that the results he obtained would be true for other groups of students—a whole population of students.

The term *population* is used to describe any group of people or observations or test items in which we happen to be interested. The population of students mentioned earlier might be defined as first-year college of education students who have come straight from school to college. To survey the work habits of this whole population would be a lengthy task—unnecessarily so. If we choose a *sample* from the population so that it has exactly the same characteristics as the population, the results obtained from the sample will, within certain limits, be the same as results which would have been obtained from the whole population. These 'certain limits' are determined by tests of statistical significance.

By chance, in the way the sample is selected, it is inevitable that slight differences between sample and population will occur. The smaller the sample, the more likely it is that the sample will produce different results from the population. Tests of statistical significance have been devised to deal with this problem by allowing for the effect of sample size on the results. Each statistical measure—$\chi^2$, correlation, mean—has its own test of significance to allow for chance variations in the sample. From these tests it is possible to estimate within what limits the true value for the population will lie—the smaller the sample, the wider the limits. If we have, for example, small samples of male and female students and find a difference in their study habits, it may well be statistically insignificant. This implies that we cannot tell whether this difference is real—implying that it would also be found in the whole population of students—or a result of choosing, by chance, unrepresentative students in the samples.

This discussion of the need for tests of statistical significance has also highlighted three important aspects of sampling: the definition of the population, the size of the sample and the need to obtain a representative sample. Each of these points must be treated carefully if the research is to be worth while.

The first task in sampling is to identify and define precisely the population to be sampled. If we are studying immigrant children, we must define the 'population' of immigrant children: what ages are included by the term 'children'; what countries are implied by 'immigrant'; whether we refer to migration from one's place of birth or merely migration from a former place of residence, and so on. Careful attention must be given to the precise limits of the population, whether or not to include individuals whose position is marginal. For example, in defining a population of primary school children, does one exclude children from independent schools, children attending special schools for the handicapped, children outside the normal age-range of primary school who happen to be at primary schools, and so on? A certain obsessional quality in respect of detail is a desirable trait in the personality of the research worker.

The second task is to estimate the appropriate numbers required for the sample. Too often, the size of the sample is decided arbitrarily: we include as many subjects as time or facilities or funds permit. As a result, findings either fail to reach significance level or they go so far beyond the significance level that much of the effort is wasted in confirming results which would have come out clearly from a much smaller sample.

Deciding on the optimum size of sample can be a complex operation, depending on preliminary estimates of probable error in the statistics to be used for analysis. A detailed explanation of the procedure and examples of the computation involved are given in chapter 6 of C. A. Moser's (1958) *Survey Methods in Social Investigation*. As a simple example, a study which is to use correlation will probably be inconclusive if it is based on less than 100 cases. For unless the correlations are all fairly high, one can make a rough estimate of the amount of random error in any one correlation coefficient on the basis of $\dfrac{1}{\sqrt{N-3}}$ (the standard error of Fisher's 'z' coefficient): with a sample of 100, a correlation coefficient is not even dependable to the first place of decimals. One in six of a series of samples taken from the same population will give results which lie outside a range of $\pm 0.1$ on either side of the true correlation. With a sample of 200, the first place of decimals becomes slightly more dependable. How many cases one needs depends on the degree of refinement sought in the correlations. Similarly, one can estimate optimum numbers for other techniques of analysis on the basis of a guess at the expected pattern of results. This can become a highly sophisticated aspect of designing experiments, and for large-scale projects or expensive test procedures (such as individual testing) it may loom large in the planning stage. Even a student project should take account of such considerations in order to avoid the disappointment of inconclusive findings and yet to economize on costs and effort where one can safely choose a smaller sample.

RANDOM SAMPLING

Finally, if the sample is to give a true measure of the whole population, it must be a representative sample. Of the many approaches to this problem the most common is that of *random sampling*, in which every individual has an equal chance of appearing in the sample. Putting all the names in a hat and picking out names for the sample is an example of random sampling. A less cumbersome method is to use a table of random numbers to select individuals from a numbered list. Lists of pupils in a class, if not in alphabetical order, are unlikely to be arranged at random. If they are in order of ability (or date of birth), selecting the first name from each of a series of classes will give a sample which is above average ability (or age); if one selects every seventh name from classes of thirty-five, the sample will be slightly below average of the 'population', that is, of all the classes.

Sampling on the basis of a factor irrelevant to the topic of research is called *systematic sampling*, and produces the equivalent of a random sample. It is sometimes difficult to be quite sure that a factor is totally irrelevant: selecting those whose name begins with M may give a sample with too many Scots, while any other letter may result in too few Scots. Whether such bias matters depends on the topic. Date of birth—especially a number of dates spread evenly over the year—provides a sound basis for obtaining a representative sample which is easy to apply to school populations. Thus, when the Scottish Mental Survey took a 1 in 60 sample of the Scottish eleven-year-old population, those who were born on the first day of an even-numbered month were selected. The survey had collected much information about the entire population, and comparison with the 1 in 60 sample showed that this method of selection had produced a sample which was a very accurate model of the whole. (The Survey also took a 1 in 10 sample, and by mistake selected those born on the first three days of any month. This unfortunately gave a sample thirteen days older than the population. The proper basis should have been those born on the 14th, 15th or 16th of any month.)

At this stage, the introduction of two further technical terms, 'sampling frame' and 'sampling ratio', may help to clarify the actual procedure involved in drawing a sample. A sampling frame, in educational research, is usually a list of all the units in the 'population' from which the sample is to be drawn: the names of the children in a school, or the complete list of schools in an area, or the census districts in a town. (It is called a 'frame' because it marks the area to be studied, and in other kinds of research, this may be an area of ground or something other than a list.) If the sampling frame includes 2,500 children, and the optimum size of sample is 250, the sampling ratio is 1/10. If possible, this should be drawn as a random sample. If the list is numbered, 250 names are drawn by taking 250 sequences (each of four digits) from a table of random numbers.

In educational research, a random sample is often an inconvenient group: two or three pupils are selected from one school, a dozen from another, and so on. *Two-stage sampling* may simplify administration, though any departure from purely random sampling complicates the analysis and introduces distorting factors into the results. In two-stage sampling, a sample of schools is taken, and within the selected schools a sample of pupils.

With *multi-stage sampling*, used in national surveys, random samples of education areas are selected—within each area a random sample of schools, within each school a random sample of classes, and so on. Provided that each individual unit in each stage has an equal chance of being selected for inclusion, a representative sample emerges which permits the maximum exploitation in analysis.

Statistical inference from such samples is obviously a complex matter. Anyone attempting sophisticated sampling procedures should consult a guide, such as H. J. Butcher's (1966) *Sampling in Educational Research*.

## STRATIFIED SAMPLING

There are other forms of sampling, and further variations on random sampling, which are described in Butcher's book and in certain statistical textbooks.

A *stratified random sample* is a variation which may be desirable in certain circumstances. For example, if a comparison of boys and girls is to be made, one can select first a sample of boys and then a sample of girls so that the proportions are equal. In a large sample, the odds are that the numbers of each sex will be approximately equal, but in a small sample—for example, twelve—it may be wise to take the precaution of stratifying by sex, that is, deciding in advance to select six boys and six girls.

Stratified sampling permits a different sampling ratio to be applied within each group. For example, if stratification by social class is thought necessary to safeguard a subsequent analysis of results by social class, one may take account of the fact that about half the population falls into social class III on the Registrar-General's Scale. If the sample is below 100, there may be too few from social classes I and II to afford accurate population estimates for this group. So a sampling ratio of 1 in 10 may be applied to social classes I and II, of 1 in 50 to social class III, and of 1 in 25 to social classes IV and V. Estimates for the total population are then got by differential weighting. It is often important to use a stratified sample in conjunction with multi-stage sampling. Samples of education areas, types of schools and varieties of classes may all have to be chosen with differing sampling ratios to ensure adequate representation in the over-all sample.

*Quota sampling* is a crude but inexpensive method similar to a stratified sample, which is commonly used in market research or opinion polls: each interviewer is given a quota to be filled— say, ten interviews with a predetermined proportion in certain age-ranges or with men and women from certain socio-economic groups. When all the results are put together, the total group of persons interviewed should be a model of the adult population in distribution of age, sex and social class.

A practical problem often arises in educational research because of children who are absent from school. When a random sample of children has been carefully drawn from a number of schools for, say, individual testing by an experienced psychologist who travels from school to school, much time will be wasted by visits to a school where the selected child is absent, or by return visits to pick up the 'left-overs' who were absent on the first visit. Since attendance rates are normally about 90 per cent, one in ten of a sample will be absent on average when the visitor calls. (Since it happens that some children tend to have recurrent absences, the proportion expected to be absent on two successive visits is considerably more than one in a hundred.) To deal with this problem, sometimes the name next on the school or class list after the absentee (or the nearest name alphabetically, or the child with the nearest date of birth) is chosen to replace the absent member of the sample.

The rules of sampling described above are often broken for practical reasons. Many educational investigations have to use small samples which are also not obtained in a random manner and may not even be representative—for example, pupils in one class or one school. In such cases it is important to obtain and report evidence on the composition of the sample, so that readers can judge how far it is representative. The mean and standard deviation of scores on a nationally standardized test give an indication of level and spread of ability in the sample; the distribution of ages, or of social class assessed from father's occupations on the Registrar-General's Scale (see chapter 7), may also be necessary as evidence by which to judge any bias in the findings. But even with such information, the conclusions drawn from small samples must be treated with caution and tests of statistical significance used before making statements concerning the results which might have been obtained in the population from which the sample has been drawn.

SUMMARY

Samples must be chosen so as to be representative of a carefully defined population. Tests of statistical significance are used to estimate population values of variables measured in a sample. The size of the sample is to some extent determined by the type of analysis to be used. Random sampling allows every individual in the population an equal chance of appearing in the sample. Variations on random sampling are systematic sampling and two-stage or multi-stage sampling. Where different sampling ratios are applied to sub-groups within the population, a stratified sample is obtained. Opinion polls use quota sampling to produce the same effect.

In many educational research projects, practical difficulties in the organization of schools prevent truly representative samples from being obtained. Here evidence must be collected showing to what extent the sample differs from the population on important measures. Without this information it is impossible to interpret from non-random samples.

## CHAPTER 4

Interviews

An important part of the planning of a research project is the choice of methods by which data are to be collected. This will influence the precise form of the hypotheses or questions to be studied and the nature of the sample to be drawn. Research findings must rest on evidence, and eight of the next nine chapters deal with techniques of gathering evidence in educational research. These include tests, inventories, attitude scales, school examinations, ratings, assessments of home background and classroom observation. The research interview and the questionnaire represent a direct method of collecting information, and are considered first. The questionnaire is best understood as an impersonal (and sometimes anonymous) version of the personal questioning of the interview. Other techniques which are discussed in later chapters may be incorporated in an interview or a questionnaire; for example, an attitude scale may comprise part of a questionnaire or a short vocabulary test may be included in an interview to provide a crude but convenient measure of ability. But it will be helpful to set out first the framework of the interview and questionnaire techniques. For a standard procedure has been developed to reduce the elements of bias and subjectivity in interviews and questionnaires, to anticipate and remove ambiguities and irrelevancies, and to ensure that the resulting data are suitable for coding, processing and analysis.

Most people associate interviews with selection. The technique of the selection interview is quite different in form and purpose from that of the research interview, and it should be made clear at the outset that the following account applies only to the research interview. In a research interview, a sample is interviewed in order to collect unbiased information in a form which permits the answers from each subject to be put together to give an accurate picture of the population from which the sample is drawn.

When is an inquiry by interview to be preferred to the use of questionnaires? The questionnaire method is too clumsy for dealing with a complex topic, where different kinds of information are sought from different groups of people. With such inquiries one cannot tell in advance which questions will be applicable to this or that group; it is much more effective to have a trained interviewer who can select the appropriate blocks of questions to be put, or check that the procedure is in fact correctly understood by the subject. Personal topics, especially questions likely to arouse emotion or embarrassment or suspicion, require either an interview approach or the use of an anonymous questionnaire. Anonymity prevents the follow-up of non-responders—it may even have the effect of encouraging non-response—and it prevents the researcher from collating the questionnaire data with other information which he has about his subjects. Filling in a questionnaire is a more detached or cold-blooded activity than responding in a live interview: this is at once both the strength and weakness of the more objective approach. Interviews are more difficult to arrange, less convenient for the sample, more expensive and time consuming. But interviews must be used with subjects who might refuse to complete or be incapable of filling in questionnaires. With a perceptive interviewer such people are more likely to give true information through an interview which has been *properly planned and conducted*.

For the research interview is not merely a matter of subjective impression or spontaneous interaction between interviewer and subject. If responses from a number of subjects are to be collated, and if results from different interviewers are to be compared or combined, all the interviews in a research project must follow a standard procedure. Clearly, an interview involves interaction: a completely standardized interview procedure would defeat the essential purpose of the interview. Yet it is possible (and necessary) to impose a considerable degree of standardization on the interview without losing spontaneity of participation by the subjects.

The basic principles of the *standardized interview* are that a

1.  I would like to ask you first about the schools ............ has been to so far.
    Did he/she go to a nursery school or nursery class?

    CODE AS 'NO-3' IF ATTENDED     PROBE    {Yes, in this country.................... 1
    NURSERY FOR LESS THAN      IF NEC. {Yes, abroad only...................... 2
    ONE MONTH IN TOTAL                 No ................................................. 3
                                              D.K. ................................................ 4

    (a) If Yes, in this country (1) **and child is now in infants:**
    Was this a nursery class in his/her **present school?**

                                             Yes .............. 1
                                             No .............. 2

2.  How old was he/she when he/she first started to go to school in the mornings and afternoons?

                                           Under $3\frac{1}{2}$ years old................. 1
                                           $3\frac{1}{2}$ years but less than 4.......... 2
    INCLUDE NURSERY SCHOOL              4 years but less than $4\frac{1}{2}$.......... 3
    OR CLASS IF ATTENDED                $4\frac{1}{2}$ years but less than 5.......... 4
    IN THE MORNINGS                       5 years but less than $5\frac{1}{2}$.......... 5
    AND AFTERNOONS                        $5\frac{1}{2}$ years but less than 6.......... 6
                                             6 or older.............................. 7
                                             D.K. ................................... 8

3.  Was that a good age for him/her to start or would you have liked him/her to have started earlier or later?

                                           Good age to start.................... 2
    THIS REFERS TO STARTING            Earlier start preferred............. 1 } ask (a)
    IN THE MORNINGS                       Later start preferred................ 3 }
    AND AFTERNOONS                       D.K./Not sure ...................... 4

    (a) If earlier/later start **preferred (1 or 3):** At what age would you
    have liked ............ to have started?

                                           Under $3\frac{1}{2}$ years old................. 1
                                           $3\frac{1}{2}$ years but less than 4.......... 2
                THIS REFERS TO MORNINGS     4 years but less than $4\frac{1}{2}$.......... 3
                AND AFTERNOONS                 $4\frac{1}{2}$ years but less than 5.......... 4
                AT SCHOOL                         5 years but less than $5\frac{1}{2}$.......... 5
                                             $5\frac{1}{2}$ years but less than 6.......... 6
                                             6 or older.............................. 7
                                             D.K. ................................... 8

49. We are interested to know what children like to do out of school, and the sort of places
    there are in the area where children can play or go to out of school.
    Apart from indoors, where does ............ play most of the time?

                                                               CODE ONE
                                                               ONLY

    ONLY ONE TO BE CODED.        Own garden/yard/play space, open
    IF PARENT CANNOT GIVE        space round/between flats.................... 1
    ONE ONLY, PRIORITY            Friends'/neighbours' garden or yard...... 2
    CODE 1 DOWNWARDS           Park, heath, common, fields................... 3
                                         {Playground, outdoor play centre, re-
                                       creation grounds, 'play' street................. 4
                                       Bombed site, car park, waste land.......... 5
                                       Street (excluding 'play' streets).............. 6
                                       D.K. ................................................ 7
                                       Other (specify)

Figure 2. Items from the Interview Schedule in the Plowden Social Survey
(Plowden Report, vol. 2, appendix 3, pp. 158 and 172)

0. **A.** I am going to read out a list of things and I would like you to tell me whether you have any of these within easy distance of your home (i.e. easy distance for a child to get to by himself/herself or, if too young, easy for a parent or other adult to take child to).

RECORD PRESENCE BY RINGING CODE IN COL. A.

**B.** Has ............ used this at all this year (i.e. SINCE THIS TIME LAST YEAR). RECORD ITEMS USED BY RINGING CODE IN COL. B.

**C.** Is there anything else that you wish there were round here for ............? RECORD BY RINGING APPROPRIATE CODE IN COL. C *OR* WRITING IN 'OTHERS' BELOW BOX.

| PROMPT LIST FOR A AND B | A. Present | B. Used | C. Wanted |
|---|---|---|---|
| | (CODE ALL THAT APPLY) | | |
| (1) A park, public garden, heath, common or fields where children are allowed to play.................... | 1 | 1 | 1 |
| (2) A proper playground or outdoor play centre (OTHER THAN SCHOOL) ............................ | 2 | 2 | 2 |
| (3) Swimming or paddling places which are safe for children ...... | 3 | 3 | 3 |
| (4) An indoor play centre................... | 4 | 4 | 4 |
| (5) Any children's clubs or societies (e.g. Cubs, Brownies, Scouts, Guides, church clubs, youth clubs for young children, sports clubs)................. | 5 | 5 | 5 |
| (6) A cinema or other place which has children's film shows ... | 6 | 6 | 6 |
| (7) A public library................................. | 7 | 7 | 7 |
| C. Other (specify) Off. Use | | | |
| | a | b | c |

1. (I realise from what you have told me that you are very busy). In the evenings when ............ comes home from school do you have any time free to do things with him/her if he/she wants you to? (Such as playing or reading with him/her, taking him/her out, showing him/her how to do things).

THIS REFERS TO WEEKDAY EVENINGS, NOT WEEKENDS.

IF YES, PROMPT 'Is this most evenings or just occasionally?'

Yes, does things with child most evenings........ ... 1
Yes, but only on occasional evenings............. ... 2
No ...................................................... ... 3

Reprinted from *Children and their Primary Schools* (the Plowden Report), H.M. Stationary Office, 1967, by permission of the Controller of Her Majesty's Stationery Office.

precise wording is determined in advance for the key questions and a preliminary classification of response is also prepared. This is the framework of the *interview schedule*. The interview schedule is prepared in considerable detail: it prescribes the pattern to be followed in the interview, sets down the wording of questions and instructions, with the necessary alternative forms to be used, and provides for the recording or categorization of answers by the persons interviewed. The interview schedule used in the National Survey of Parental Attitudes and Circumstances for the Plowden Committee is reproduced in twenty pages of small print of the Report, *Children and their Primary Schools* (volume 2, appendix 3). Figure 2 pp. 34 and 35 shows part of this interview schedule.

The labour in constructing an interview schedule is considerable. The research worker is usually in a hurry to start, and if he alone is doing the interviewing he will be tempted to rush the stages of construction and trial. Inadequate preparation may be disastrous, as, for example, when the interviewer discovers half-way through his sample that there is an ambiguity in his questions or a key point which he has omitted. By then it will be too late to check back with those whom he has already interviewed, even if that were possible without bias in the results.

## PREPARATION OF THE SCHEDULE

The first stages in the procedure for constructing an interview schedule resemble the initial stages in 'planning research', described in chapter 2. Stage 1 is preparation. This starts with the reading of previous studies on the subject, or related aspects of the subject, from the point of view of the proposed interview, in order to note points to explore. The researcher specifies more precisely in his mind (or on paper) the aims of his inquiry, formulates hypotheses about the important factors in his area of study, and designs tentative questions (or other methods of collecting information) to explore these factors and test his hypotheses.

If, for example, he wished to study the recruitment of teachers, and this topic had been more precisely defined as a study of attitudes of undergraduates to teaching as a career, he will find previous studies which claim to explain these attitudes in different ways. Some studies concentrate on identifying aspects of teaching which are attractions or deterrents to the choice of teaching as a career. Others treat the topic in terms of the roles which students seek for themselves and which they ascribe to teachers. Others again focus on personality qualities in the student, or use attitude scales and indirect questions in inventory form as a means of exploring basic personality factors. From all these, a selection must be made and an emphasis (or series of emphases) must be decided. An omission at this stage cannot be remedied later. Reviewing previous work is the surest way of covering a wide range of possibilities.

As was noted in chapter 2, this initial stage is a period of stress for the would-be researcher. It is a stage of mental uncertainty— the person who is not open to doubts can hardly hope to be successful in research except by brilliant intuition. Intuitions are necessary, but they must be viewed critically and sceptically. Reading other people's reports can be demoralizing, for inevitably these show that the problem is more complicated than was realized. Previous work seems either so extensive that there is nothing more to be done, or it is so scanty and inadequate that there is no worth-while guide to action. Or you discover a previous study which has already covered the aspect which you thought was a new and original approach. A certain strength of personality is needed to survive this stage, and to tackle it thoroughly.

Stage 2 completes the preparatory work. The population to be sampled, and the sampling procedure, must be decided and defined precisely in one of the ways already described in chapter 3. A provisional content of the interview must also be decided. The points to be explored in the course of the interview are arranged in a sequence which will allow the interview to flow naturally from point to point. It is usually wise to begin with factual questions and simple topics, to help establish rapport by an easy interchange of conversation between interviewer and subject.

Complex questions come later, and questions which might cause even the slightest embarrassment or hostility (which would affect replies to subsequent questions) should be left till near the end. After the sequence has been decided, the specific questions are framed, with the precise wording written out in full. Two points should be noted in framing the questions. First, be careful to use words which all the subjects will be sure to understand. Avoid technical jargon, and remember that already the topic is far more familiar to you than it is to the persons you are to interview. Shortcuts of thought and expression quickly become established in the mind: what is needed is the teacher's skill of seeing a problem through the eyes of both expert and novice. Secondly, the wording of questions must not introduce a bias by favouring one form of answer rather than another. This is an obvious point, but it is not as easy as it might be thought to detect bias in a question. 'Do you agree that . . .?' is a question encouraging a 'Yes' response. 'Do you believe that . . .?' 'Do you support those who believe that . . .?' 'Would you be prepared to say that . . .?' There are many ways of asking for expression of an attitude, and it is difficult to say which of them is neutral. Use of an attitude scale (chapter 12) may be the answer.

An interview schedule need not (and should not) be restricted to question and answer. Rating scales, check lists or attitude scales may be included to give an objective measure on some point; a long interview may be broken by a short interval in which the subject records certain information with paper and pencil; even a short test may sometimes be included. The construction of an attitude scale or other similar measure for a specific aspect of the inquiry involves certain procedures (described in chapters 11 and 12), including pilot studies independently of the pilot run for the interview schedule.

PILOT RUN

We now have a provisional draft of the interview schedule. Stage 3 is the *pilot run*, to try out the provisional sequence of points or questions. There is a strong temptation to limit this to a trial on a couple of friends, or even to omit this stage altogether. To do this is usually a disastrous mistake. The pilot run is done with a sample which is similar to the group from whom the interview sample will be selected, but obviously it must not include any who will be interviewed later.

When the pilot sample is interviewed, answers are recorded as fully as possible. Serious faults in the structure of the interview can be modified as they are discovered, but usually it is best to give the provisional sequence of questions a fair run without trying to make changes for what may be an untypical subject among the first two or three interviewed. It is sometimes useful at this stage to make tape-recordings of these interviews. This will allow a check to be made on the style of the interviewer, and it will also be easier to detect flaws in the design of the schedule.

At the end of this pilot run, the questions and responses are examined to remedy omissions, possibly to revise the order of questions, and principally to identify ambiguities or points where there has been confusion. Ambiguities may be removed by a change of word or addition of an explanation. Sometimes it is necessary to insert prompts or probes. These are additional questions which an interviewer may use at his discretion to press his main question (prompt) or to clarify the reply (probe). They should be written into the interview schedule at the appropriate point after the questions, so that the same wording is used in each case. Note the neutral form of the wording in the following examples:*

Question: What occupation do you intend to enter after you have graduated?

Prompt: If the student says 'It depends on what degree I get,' then say, 'Assuming you get the kind of degree you are expecting at the moment'.

Probe: If the student says 'Post-graduate study', say, 'What type of study do you have in mind?'

* Taken from the interview schedule used in MORTON-WILLIAMS, R., FINCH, S. and POLL, C. (1966) *Undergraduates' Attitudes to School Teaching as a Career*, Social Survey Report, 354. Mimeographed.

Further examples of the use of prompts will be found in figure 2.

If the changes involved in this revision are substantial, a further pilot run may be necessary, though possibly on a smaller scale, as a check. Otherwise the final form and sequence of the questions are now determined, and the interview schedule is beginning to take shape, though it is not yet complete. The questions are ready, but we must consider how to record and classify the responses.

## PREPARATION OF A CODING SYSTEM

Stage 4 of the procedure reviews the responses in the pilot run. These give an indication of the probable range of answers to be expected, and provide a basis for a system of recording and classifying the answers to each question. Recording answers in full is clumsy, interferes with rapport and wastes time. (Recording on tape, and employing a typist to make a transcript, is practicable in the pilot run, but material accumulates unmanageably if this method is attempted during the main run of interviews in a survey.) Generally, classifying and recording responses are best done simultaneously. If a sound system of classifying responses can be worked out in advance on the basis of the pilot run, so that each of the more frequent responses is represented by a number, the majority of the actual responses during the main run can be recorded merely by circling the appropriate number. It is of little use collecting information in a form which cannot be used in the analysis, or recording in full certain infrequent responses which will be grouped in a general category when the replies are collated. This principle of *coding* responses has wider application than merely a technique of grouping: often the question is framed in such a way as to facilitate coding, for this makes the question more precise. For example, in the Social Survey inquiry into teachers' recruitment, which was referred to earlier, a question on salary asked, 'What do you think is the starting salary (of a teacher) in a State school for a graduate with a good Honours degree?' The range of replies from undergraduates in the pilot run was from £300 a year to £3,000. In the Social Survey interviews students were given a card with a range of salaries from which they selected an appropriate reply to the question. The code number for that response was entered by the interviewer on the interview schedule.

In short, stage 4 may be summarized as the preparation of a coding system, a topic which is included in the discussion on data processing in chapter 6. Here it is sufficient merely to describe the standard practice. This is to design a lay-out of the interview schedule which permits all the answers to be recorded and checked easily—for example, in a margin on the right-hand side of the page, spaced to correspond with the questions opposite, but numbered to correspond with the columns in the punched cards which will be used in the processing of data (see figure 2). This arrangement is economic of time and labour, and reduces the risk of errors in transferring information from the interview schedules to the cards or whatever simpler device is used for handling the data in the analysis process. Thus the interviewer can now use one copy of his schedule for each interview, recording in the margin in coded form the responses, opinions and attitudes expressed by the subject. In this way, the rapport of the interview is maintained, since the interviewer is not obviously copying down responses word for word, but accuracy of recording is ensured since the replies are coded and checked as the subject speaks, and not marked afterwards from memory.

Finally, before sending the schedule to be printed or duplicated, you must go over the wording of questions again for a further check on prompts or probes which may be necessary.

CONDUCTING THE INTERVIEWS

The whole of this chapter so far has been concerned with the drawing up of the interview schedule. There is also the matter of conducting the interviews. Large surveys employ professional interviewers; small-scale ones cannot afford to be amateurish. The organization of a programme of interviews will certainly run into problems, but most of them can be anticipated by good sense and careful planning. Interview technique is a skill which requires training and practice. The importance of technique should not be underrated, and the use of a tape-recorder in rehearsals and the aid of a frank colleague helps even the most confident of us to discover flaws in our manner. The cardinal rule is to follow the 'script' of the interview schedule in a natural manner, adapting the links between questions but presenting each item in the standard form. All amateur interviewers talk when they should listen (a fault of more than interviewers).

At the start the main task is to establish rapport, to make contact and allow the subject to feel at ease. It is even more difficult to sustain this easy relation throughout the interview. Some interviewers, of course, can do this more easily than others, and careful observation of a skilled interviewer will improve one's own technique. He looks at the person he is interviewing, in fairly short and frequent glances and not fixedly, records discreetly, sustains conversation in a neutral way by repeating the last statement of the other person in a slightly different form with an interrogative intonation, is not distracted by irrelevancies, has polite and easy techniques for coming back to the point and for stopping a garrulous flow, and so on. At the end of the interview, time must be left to allow the interviewer to check that he has marked a response to every item, while he can still recall the answer for any which he has accidentally omitted.

Some of those asked to attend for interview will fail to turn up. A check on these must be made. As the procedure involved resembles that used for non-responders to a questionnaire, this aspect will be dealt with in the next chapter.

While the structured interview is widely used because the data collected can easily be collated and analysed, it may be inappropriate for use on certain complex problems or with certain groups of people. It restricts the freedom of the individual to develop his own reasoned arguments. Where the interviewer is hoping to glean new insight on a problem from someone who has wide experience, the free interview planned to cover certain important areas but otherwise unstructured, may be useful. With this type of interview the use of a tape-recorder will allow a transcript of the interview to be made. A later analysis of the discussion will ensure that the research worker uses the interviewee's experience or expertise to best advantage. The disadvantages of the unstructured interview will still have to be faced. If a series of such interviews has been conducted, it is unlikely that the discussions will overlap sufficiently to allow comparisons to be made. The responses cannot be coded and no quantitative assessment of attitudes or opinions will be possible.

SUMMARY

The research interview is designed to collect comparable data from all those interviewed. This can only be achieved if the interview is carefully structured and standardized by use of a schedule. By following this schedule different interviewers will ask exactly the same questions in the same order, thus ensuring that the responses will have been obtained under comparable conditions.

The questions to be asked are decided after a search of the pertinent literature. A pilot study provides evidence of possible ambiguities or inappropriate questions. This trial run also allows categories of response to be decided, which are incorporated in the main interview schedule as numbers or symbols to be circled. Such pre-coding of the schedule allows the interviewer to record replies easily without interrupting the rapport. Tape-recordings of the trial interviews also help to warn the interviewer of faulty style. He may be talking too much himself or failing to sustain conversation in a neutral yet natural manner.

## CHAPTER 5

Questionnaires

The questionnaire may be regarded as a form of interview on paper. Procedure for the construction of a questionnaire follows a pattern similar to that of the interview schedule. However, because the questionnaire is impersonal, it is all the more important to take care over its construction. Since there is no interviewer to explain ambiguities or to check misunderstandings, the questionnaire must be especially clear in its wording. The variety of possible answers to each question must be anticipated more fully than for an interview. The pilot run for a questionnaire is thus of special importance. The skill of an interviewer can sometimes redeem minor defects in an interview schedule; but one single flaw in a questionnaire may provide the respondent with a justification for committing it to the waste-paper basket.

One main weakness of the questionnaire method is that inevitably a proportion of the sample will not answer, and it is difficult to discover why, or to discover how the non-responders differ from those who do reply. Consequently, the percentage response is the most important single consideration in evaluating a questionnaire study; and some attempt to estimate the opinions of non-responders is an important part of the inquiry by questionnaire, one which is neglected more often than not.

The obvious advantage in using questionnaires rather than interview is economy in cost, time and labour. The fact that questionnaires are impersonal can sometimes be turned to advantage—for example, when answers are given anonymously. But for the most part questionnaire responses should be treated with caution and the questionnaire method should be used only for relatively simple and factual inquiries, although it may form a necessary part of more complex studies. Complex questions may be answered superficially, and some people will refuse to answer questions which involve difficult choices or which permit an unflattering interpretation. People may throw away a questionnaire rather than risk showing themselves at a disadvantage. For this reason it is false optimism for the researcher to think that he can conceal his reason for asking certain questions. He must expect his sample to be suspicious and on guard. Even 'captive' samples, such as students in a class, find ingenious ways of avoiding questions which, rightly or wrongly, they interpret as threatening.

Questionnaires to schools are so numerous nowadays—and so often a nuisance when they are loosely or ambiguously or inappropriately worded—that special care must be taken if you hope to win an adequate response. A first rule is to secure permission from the appropriate authority to circulate your questions. (Advice on this point is given in the appendix, p. 177 ff.) In self-defence against time-wasting inquiries, many authorities have issued a ruling that no unauthorized questionnaires are to be answered.

CHOOSING THE QUESTIONS

Stage 1 in a questionnaire inquiry is to define the problem precisely. This involves reading widely, as was described for stage 1 in the preparation of an interview schedule. It is desirable also to define at an early stage the population to whom the questionnaire is to be directed and to decide the nature of the sample to be drawn, as this may influence the drafting of the questionnaire. The definition of the problem should set out one by one the aspects of the problem to be explored; and stage 2 follows on from this with the construction of questions or items to deal with each aspect in turn. For this, a pre-pilot study may be helpful, in which open-ended questions are put to a group whose co-operation you can count on, in order to discover the variety of possible answers or responses. Note that the procedure is to define the aspects to be covered and then to frame questions or items to deal with these, not to make up questions and then consider what interpretations can be wrung from them. Here, as before, the questions should be compiled with definite hypotheses or theories in mind. Each question should contribute clear information on a specific aspect to be explored—or else the question should be discarded ruthlessly.

If the investigation is on a small scale and the investigator himself will classify all the responses, it may not be necessary to put all questions into a multiple-choice pattern. Multiple-choice can be tiresome, especially if the alternatives offered for choice do not express adequately the response a subject wishes to express. Open questions, if they are included, must not be too general or they will be unclassifiable, and should be restricted to fairly straightforward topics where answers can easily be coded subsequently. A multiple-choice structure which includes the option 'Other (please specify)' may be a suitable compromise, though it is a sign of bad construction if this option is chosen at all frequently in the replies.

If the investigation is on a relatively large scale, involving the analysis of replies from, say, 300 or more persons, then the form in which questions are put must take account of how the answers are to be classified and coded. As was explained in the previous chapter, information from large numbers can be used only so far as it can be classified. Accurate comparisons of response become impossible otherwise. Consequently, it may be necessary to choose questions and to specify possible answers in such a way as to facilitate coding. The art of drafting a questionnaire consists of being able to do this without forcing your respondents into an uneasy choice—a difficulty which they can too easily resolve by giving up altogether. Ideally it should be possible to code the responses (that is, to transform them into numbers for punching on a card) directly from the questionnaire itself, to reduce the risk of errors in transferring the information on to an intermediate coding sheet. As with the interview schedule, responses should be recorded down the right-hand margin. The most convenient arrangement when the data are to be transferred to punched cards is to use numbers corresponding to alternative answers, the appropriate number to be circled. It is not necessary to rule off

the margin with the forbidding heading 'For official use only';
skilful lay-out should produce the desired arrangement without
resort to complicated instructions. It is neither wise nor fair to
leave the typist or the printer with this important task of deciding
spacing and alignment.

The questionnaire should start with simple factual questions,
so that the person completing it gets off to a good start. Complex
or awkward topics should come towards the end. An open-ended
general question at the end will allow expression of points which
the responder thinks important, though they are not covered by
the questionnaire.

A questionnaire need not be restricted to questions: attitude
scales, ratings and check lists may be included, providing they are
brief and straightforward and the instructions are kept simple.
Simplicity and brevity are cardinal virtues. In a check list (in
which the responder is asked to check the items which apply to
him), it may be necessary to specify the number of items to be
checked ('Mark the *three* reasons which you think are the most
important'); or, alternatively, to recognize that it will be difficult
to classify responses. Adding the number of times an item is
checked assumes that each check is equivalent, and this assumption
is probably invalid when one person marks almost every item
on a list and another picks out only one.

These warnings represent relatively minor problems in the
framing of questions, compared with the danger of wording
questions so that you get back the answers which you expect or
which you would like to get. Results inevitably will be biased if
the questions give even a hint of which answer is likely to be
preferred. This point has been emphasized in the previous
chapter and it deserves repetition here.

The distinction between a leading question and a neutral
question is sometimes difficult to decide. For example, which of
the following is a neutral wording?

Are you in favour of abolishing corporal punishment?
Should corporal punishment be abolished?
Should corporal punishment be retained?
Is it practicable to abolish corporal punishment?

QUESTIONNAIRE

SECTION A. PERSONAL DETAILS

(i) In which type of school are you at present employed?

| | | |
|---|---|---|
| Infant .. .. | I | |
| Infant/Junior .. | 2 | |
| Junior .. .. | 3 | |
| Secondary Modern | 4 | |
| Other Secondary | 5 | |

} Col. 12

(ii) By which LEA are you at present employed?

LEAVE BLANK

............................ | | | | Cols 13/14/15

(iii) Sex

| | |
|---|---|
| Man | I |
| Woman | 2 |

} Col. 16

(iv) What is your age in years? .. .. | | | Cols 17/18

(v) What is your present grade?

| | |
|---|---|
| Head Teacher | I |
| Assistant Teacher | 2 |

} Col. 19

(vi) What is your qualification?

| | |
|---|---|
| Teacher's Certificate .. | I |
| Trained Graduate .. | 2 |
| Untrained Graduate .. | 3 |
| Unqualified .. .. | 4 |

} Col. 20

Figure 3. Questionnaire to teachers providing information for the Plowden Committee (Plowden Report, vol. 2, appendix 1, pp. 4 and 5)

SECTION B. ORGANISATION OF PRIMARY EDUCATION

1. Should all children enter school at the beginning of the school
   year?

| | | |
|---|---|---|
| YES | 1 | |
| NO | 2 | |
| UND | 3 | |

} Col. 21

2. Should nursery education

   (*a*) be available only for those with special
   needs?  ..  ..  ..  .. ___1___

   (*b*) be available for all children whose
   parents wish it?  ..  ..  .. ___2___ } Col. 22

   (*c*) not be available?  ..  ..  .. ___3___

   Undecided ..  ..  ..  .. ___4___

3. Should nursery education be part-time for most children?

| | | |
|---|---|---|
| YES | 1 | |
| NO | 2 | |
| UND | 3 | |

} Col. 23

4. If you think nursery education should be generally available,
   should this be from

   age 2?  .. ___2___

   age 3?  .. ___3___ } Col. 24

   age 4?  .. ___4___

   Undecided .. ___5___

Reprinted from *Children and their Primary Schools* (the Plowden Report), H.M.
Stationery Office, 1967, by permission of the Controller of Her Majesty's
Stationery Office.

Each of these, in its own way, contains some element of direction to which the respondent may react. It will be almost impossible to obtain completely neutral questions, but it is essential to avoid the more obvious leading questions. Besides being neutral, the question must avoid making the person feel inadequate in any way. The interview schedule from the Plowden Social Survey provides a model of careful wording.

12. Was your husband able to take much interest in which school (your child) went to or did he leave that to you?
26. Do you feel quite happy about the methods of teaching used at (PRESENT SCHOOL) and the way (your child) is getting on in his/her work, or is there anything which worries you at all?
37. On the whole do the teachers seem to treat all the children pretty fairly or not?
55. Do you ever manage to go for outings together as a family?
60. If you (or your husband) have any time for relaxing, do you do any reading?

As an example of the lay-out and working of a simple questionnaire, figure 3 shows some of the questions put to some 3,000 teachers to collect evidence used in the Plowden Report (volume 2, appendix 1).

INTRODUCTORY LETTER

At the end of stage 2, a provisional draft of the questionnaire is now ready. In stage 3, the letter to accompany and explain the questionnaire must be prepared. The wording of this letter should be studied as carefully as the wording of the questionnaire itself, for this is the means by which the sample must be persuaded to co-operate. The letter should first explain the reason for the inquiry. This reason should be expressed in terms of values which are relevant to the sample—*not* on the lines of 'I am writing a thesis on . . .', but emphasizing instead the use or importance of the information asked for. A sentence on the importance of the respondent's own contribution is also appropriate. A good example of a covering letter, with suggestions for drafting, may be found in W. R. Borg's (1963) *Educational Research: An Introduction*, pp. 213-17. But whether or not you can persuade your sample to return the questionnaire will depend on the over-all impression of the letter. A neat letter, with a letter-head, personally signed and addressed, personal in style but not familiar or chatty, suggesting a date for return and enclosing a stamped addressed envelope—all this will not compensate for inadequacies in the questionnaire itself, but at least it will give your questions the chance they deserve (or should deserve).

PILOT STUDY

In stage 4, the provisional draft of the questionnaire is pre-tested on a pilot group similar to the sample to whom the questionnaire will be given. This is an essential stage, which must never be omitted through pressure of time. However much care has gone into stage 2, the pilot run will show up flaws and ambiguities, and it provides an invaluable check on the options in multiple-choice items and on the feasibility of the proposed procedure for coding responses.

These stages complete the preparatory work. Stage 5 is distribution, though the clerical labour of addressing envelopes will have begun as soon as the sample was defined. The expense of including a stamped addressed envelope is always justified. The questionnaires should be sent out at a time of year when the sample is likely to have time to deal with them—obviously not at holiday times or (for students and teachers) in the examination season. A number of replies will come promptly. When the returns begin to drop off, a brief but polite reminder will bring in a few more. A second reminder, enclosing a further copy of the questionnaire 'In case you have mislaid the original', is always worth sending, since it will add a few replies. The general run of experience is that further reminders after this seldom justify the expense.

By the end of this stage of the inquiry, the percentage response to the inquiry is known. What is an acceptable percentage? This depends on the nature of your inquiry, the accessibility of the sample, and the scarcity of comparable information from other studies. A response rate of less than 70 per cent generally implies that the findings lack validity for general application, for it means that about one in three of the sample have been missed, and this is too large a proportion to ignore. Even with a 70 per cent response, or better, there still remains an important stage 6 in the procedure, necessary in every study but of special value when the response has been disappointing. In this stage, the non-responders are the subject of a follow-up study. This has two parts. First, from any factual information already available on the sample, a statistical check is made to test how the responders differ from the non-responders—for example, in age, sex, qualifications, address, or whatever categories of analysis are available. If it is possible to identify separately those who have not received the questionnaire because of a change of address, and those who must be presumed to have received it and have declined to answer, the two groups should be studied separately. This analysis of non-responders gives some indication of the nature of the bias introduced by the incomplete returns. Secondly, a further attempt should be made to contact a sample of those who have not replied. A relatively small sample can be selected for this pursuit of the difficult customers, so that a really concentrated effort can be directed to tracing them and obtaining some indication of their general attitude to the topic of inquiry. For example, in a student question-naire study within a college, it is practicable to contact a 1 in 10 sample of non-responders personally, and by interview to check their answers to key questions. The aim in this final stage is to establish how far those who have replied are representative of the total group. But if numbers are adequate, and if all the 1 in 10 sample of non-responders have been tracked down, it may be permissible to combine the responses, weighting the answers from the sample of non-responders by a factor of ten. This is far from a perfect solution, but it does help to diminish the bias which invalidates results in the majority of questionnaire studies. In practice it may be very difficult to obtain a 70 per cent response rate from certain groups of people. Head-teachers, college principals or managers in industry may well be too busy. Smaller percentages of response can still be useful, but only where evidence of the characteristics of the non-responders has been collected and carefully assessed.

When the results are written up, any school or organization which has helped in the investigation should be given a brief summary of the findings.

The matter of interpreting data from interviews and questionnaires has not been considered in these chapters, which are concerned with techniques of design and administration. The weaknesses of questionnaires which have already been stressed mean that extreme care must be taken in the interpretation of the results from even a carefully designed questionnaire. Some of the pitfalls will be mentioned in chapter 15.

## SUMMARY

Flexner (1930) wrote in *Universities, American, English, German:* 'The questionnaire is not a scientific instrument. It is a cheap, easy and rapid method of obtaining information or non-information, one never knows which' (p. 125). He pinpoints the weakness of both questionnaire and interview—the untested validity of the responses. Questionnaires show what people say, not what they do or are. Also the virtual impossibility of posing a completely neutral question must bias the results. Any form of question implies a certain frame of reference and thereby influences the answer given. These inherent defects can, however, be minimized by taking great care in designing the questionnaires—checking the wording meticulously, using pilot studies and reminder letters, and finally identifying the non-responders.

| Data Processing

The previous two chapters have introduced techniques used for collecting data, and have emphasized the need to plan in advance how such information is to be classified. In questionnaire surveys in particular it is all too easy to collect a vast quantity of data without any clear idea of how to make sense of it afterwards. Test scores, school examination marks, personality ratings, and scores on inventories are forms of measurement which will be described later. Interpretation of such scores is generally impossible until they have been condensed into tabular form by data-processing techniques. The various methods available for condensing and systematizing the information collected are discussed under five headings:

Ledger method
Written cards
Hand-sorted punched cards
Mechanically-sorted punched cards
Computer input punched cards

The choice of a particular method will depend mainly on the size of the sample, the number of variables measured and the facilities locally available.

LEDGER METHOD

This is the mark-book method with which teachers are all too familiar. Individual names are written in the left-hand column and against these names columns of scores (or comments) are compiled. This is certainly the simplest method of handling data, and is suitable where small numbers are involved and little statistical analysis is expected. It is, however, most inflexible. If three classes of children had taken six tests, mean scores could easily be calculated for each class. But correlations between the tests would necessitate repeated copying of the appropriate columns of numbers. The ledger method has only limited use in educational research, though it is often used in addition to other methods to provide a basic 'register' for ready access to the code numbers by which individuals are identified in a large-scale project.

WRITTEN CARDS

This method is appropriate for small-scale investigations with samples of up to about 250 on which not more than about fifteen measures have been obtained. A small card is written out for each individual which contains a summary of that person's scores or responses. The card must be small enough to allow hand sorting, but large enough to allow the figures to be clearly seen. Cards of 3 × 2 or 4 × 3 in. would be suitable. Figure 4 (p. 56) shows an example of the lay-out of data on such a card. In designing the lay-out of these cards, the *identification data*—name, school and class in the example—are written in the centre of the card with the scores in boxes around the perimeter. To aid sorting, the figures should be fairly large and it is often helpful to use different colours. These cards show the person's scores at a glance and they can also be sub-divided into categories with ease. In figure 4 the sex of each pupil has been recorded by cutting off (female) the top right-hand corner of the card.

A simple analysis might be to investigate the possibility of sex differences in the mean scores on the verbal reasoning quotients (VRQ). It is usually easier to calculate means from grouped data. The categories must first be defined, using perhaps fourteen divisions as follows: 130+, 129–125, 124–120, . . ., 74–70, 69—. The cards would be divided into two packs by sex. Each pack would then be sorted into the fourteen categories providing two frequency distributions from which means and standard deviations could be calculated.

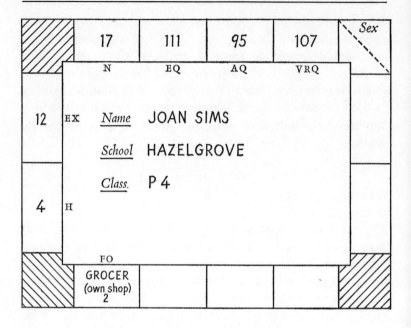

*Key*

| | | | |
|---|---|---|---|
| N | Neuroticism | VRQ | Verbal reasoning quotient |
| EX | Extraversion | AQ | Arithmetic quotient |
| H | Home | EQ | English Quotient |
| FO | Father's occupation | | |

Figure 4. Written card

## TABLE I

### CORRELATIONAL MATRIX OF TEST SCORES

| Test | 1 | 2 | 3 | 4 |
|---|---|---|---|---|
| 1. Verbal reasoning | – | | | |
| 2. Arithmetic | 0·75 | – | | |
| 3. English | 0·83 | 0·78 | – | |
| 4. Neuroticism | −0·21 | 0·27 | −0·13 | – |
| 5. Extraversion | 0·01 | −0·05 | 0·04 | −0·17 |

A more complex analysis might involve the intercorrelations between the five test scores shown in figure 4. Eventually we would aim to form a correlational 'matrix', such as that shown in table 1. To produce such a matrix it is necessary to form a *scattergram* or grid for each of the ten intercorrelations using a two-dimensional sort. The cards are first sorted into the fourteen categories of the first test. The cards in each of these categories are then sorted on the second variable into a further fourteen categories to form a 14 × 14 correlation grid from which the correlation coefficient can be calculated (Lewis, 1967, pp. 52–6).

Before starting the series of sorts described above it is important to decide on the most economical method of sorting. A *sorting schedule* is devised. In the example used in table 1, the first step would be to sort the cards vertically to form a column of fourteen verbal reasoning categories and then horizontally to form fourteen rows using the categories of the arithmetic test. After counting each of the 14 × 14 = 196 piles, the cards would be pushed back into the vertical (verbal reasoning) categories and re-sorted horizontally into the categories of the English test. This procedure continues until the cards have been sorted on the extraversion test. They would then be pushed up leaving a horizontal row of cards in the extraversion categories, which can be immediately sorted vertically into arithmetic categories. The

TABLE 2

SORTING SCHEDULE TO COMPUTE A CORRELATIONAL
MATRIX

| Test | 1 | 2 | 3 | 4 |
|------|------|------|------|------|
| 1. Verbal reasoning | – | | | |
| 2. Arithmetic | Sort 1 | – | | |
| 3. English | Sort 2 | Sort 10 | – | |
| 4. Neuroticism | Sort 3 | Sort 9 | Sort 8 | – |
| 5. Extraversion | Sort 4 | Sort 5 | Sort 6 | Sort 7 |

complete sorting schedule is shown as table 2. Sorting in this order prevents any repetition of sorts already carried out.

Following this sorting schedule also allows immediate checks on the accuracy of counting to be made. Totalling the number of cards in each row produces a frequency distribution on the vertical variable. In sorts 1 to 4 in table 2, for example, this will produce the frequency distribution on the verbal reasoning test. This vertical distribution must be the same for each of these four sorts. It is also possible to locate a mistake in sorting by comparing both vertical and horizontal distributions with the same distributions obtained in previous sorts. This checking procedure is most important, and should also be used when the sorting and counting has been done by machine. Even machines miscount on occasions!

HAND–SORTED PUNCHED CARDS

This is the first stage in mechanizing data processing procedures. The most common type of hand-sorted punched cards (figure 5) are supplied by the Copeland-Chatterson Co. Ltd (Cope-Chat Works, Dudbridge, Stroud, Gloucestershire). These cards have holes punched around the perimeter and come in various sizes. The cards are clipped in such a way that the hole then reaches the edge of a card. With a pack of these cards, a needle is pushed through a particular hole. The pack is shaken gently and the cards which have been clipped in this position fall out and can be counted. This method speeds up the sorting process considerably, but the data have to be coded before being transferred to these cards. With the written cards it was possible to write the actual scores into the boxes. With these 'Cope-Chat' cards each hole represents a category. Each hole must be numbered and assigned to a particular category of a given test, thus producing a *coding schedule* such as that shown in table 3. From the coding schedule a card is punched for each individual from the raw scores or by first preparing a *coding sheet* for each individual. The coding sheet would contain the identification data followed by a list of

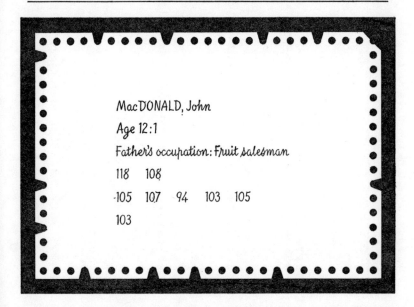

Figure 5. Hand sorted punched card

TABLE 3

CODING SCHEDULE FOR COPE-CHAT CARD

| Hole number | Variable | Category |
|---|---|---|
| I | School class | Primary 3 |
| 2 | ,, ,, | Primary 4 |
| 3 | ,, ,, | Primary 5 |
| 4 | Sex | Male (No punch= female) |
| 5 | Verbal reasoning | 130+ |
| 6 | ,, ,, | 129–125 |
| 7 | ,, ,, | 124–120 |
| 8 | ,, ,, | 119–115 |
| 9 | ,, ,, | 114–110 |
| | | etc. |

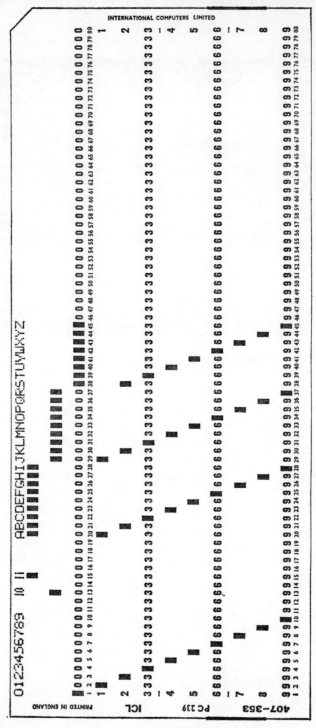

Figure 6. A machine-sorted punched card used as part of a computer input. Reprinted by permission of International Computers Ltd.

numbers representing the holes. Appropriate numbers would be circled to indicate that these holes should be clipped.

As before a sorting schedule should be designed to decide the most efficient order for sorting. Given a sorting schedule and coding sheets, the punching and sorting can be left to a clerk. This is a distinct advantage for this method of data processing, where clerical assistance can be obtained.

Hand-sorted punched cards are useful for up to about 1,000 cases, but with such large numbers the needle becomes difficult to manage and counting is laborious. The number of variables recorded is limited by the number of holes on the card and the number of categories required in each variable.

MACHINE-SORTED PUNCHED CARDS

These are plain cards which can be punched by machine in one or more of twelve positions in up to eighty columns (see figure 6). These cards can thus store a large amount of information in a small space. Again the data must be coded prior to punching. A coding schedule is prepared and the 0 to 9 positions with (X and Y) on the card conveniently permit the use of ten or twelve categories in coding. This allows a large amount of information to be put on each card. Coding sheets are produced for each individual but, for these cards, the column number is followed by the code number to be punched in that column. Punching of the cards can be done by a commercial computer agency and each punching is verified. This checking process is done by a different operator to ensure accuracy. The computer agency is also provided with a sorting schedule specifying which columns are to be sorted against which other columns. The sorting is carried out rapidly by a machine which sends the card along a moving belt and drops it into one of twelve pockets, as determined by the position of the hole in that column. The machine also counts the number of cards falling into each pocket and so can rapidly build up a correlation grid or scattergram by repeated sorting.

Until comparatively recently this was the most effective way of processing data from large samples. It still retains the advantage that the research worker can pick out a card as it drops into an unexpected category and check it. But it takes a considerable time to form a large correlational matrix and the research worker is left with the chore of working out the results from the grids by calculating machine. The type of mechanical hand-calculating machine increasingly being used in schools is the simplest and cheapest available for this purpose, but for repeated calculations it is slow and laborious. Mechanical calculating machines operated by electricity speed up these procedures, but they are noisy and slow compared with modern electronic calculators. The more expensive of these inventions are capable not only of doing instantaneous squaring and square rooting, but can also be programmed to do all the steps required in obtaining, say, a correlation coefficient. With these machines an instruction card is generally fed into the machine, the data are fed in by depressing the appropriate keys, and the machine produces the answer within a fraction of a second.

The advantages of watching the mechanical sorting and counting of cards are lost when the whole procedure of data processing and calculation of results is completed by computer. For large samples with many variables the modern computer nevertheless provides the best solution to problems of data processing.

## COMPUTER INPUT PUNCHED CARDS

Most large computers accept instructions and data in the form of magnetic tape, punched paper tape or punched cards. Punched cards are a particularly useful method of sorting educational data, as an individual card can easily be isolated and examined. This is impossible with data on tape.

A computer is capable of carrying out the data processing and also calculating the results. If a questionnaire is pre-coded (see chapter 5), the questionnaires can be sent to the computer centre and the data cards are prepared directly from these. Other forms of data will require coding sheets as before. There are programs available to do most of the sorting, counting and statistical calculations required in educational research (Hallworth, 1965). A *program* instructs the computer how to operate on the symbols punched on the data cards. The research worker will have to prepare his coding scheme to fit the program specifications, which indicate restrictions on the way in which the data may be presented to the computer. Also included in the specifications will be a way of indicating variables in terms of column numbers on the cards. These definitions allow the computer to print out tables of results correctly labelled with the names of the variables included in the analysis. Finally the specifications will contain instructions as to which tables of results are required.

Using good existing programs, with accurate punching and with correct specifications to the program, data-processing problems rapidly vanish. Much time will be wasted if data are collected first, before looking for a program to do the analysis. If the data do not match the program specifications exactly, delays will occur while the complex programs are rewritten to allow for the differences. It is also crucial to ensure that the punching has been done accurately. Inaccurate punching will introduce random errors into the data, which may prevent any significant findings emerging.

Instruction in the preparation of data for existing programs, including an introduction to computer languages such as ALGOL or FORTRAN, would now seem to be an indispensable part of the training of an educational research worker. (A straightforward introduction to ALGOL will be found in *Programming in ALGOL* (Ministry of Aviation, 1964).) It is useful to be able to read descriptions of existing computer programs so as to decide on the most appropriate way to code data before using computer programs. The research worker should also know where appropriate programs may be obtained.

Modern data processing bears little resemblance to the primitive approaches of the mark-book or written card. But the computer cannot manufacture good results out of poor data. Knowledge, flexibility of mind, good design and attention to detail are still the basis of sound research. To use sophisticated machinery on small-scale studies is wasteful when the data can be sorted manually. Even in large-scale studies, inspection of raw data and some manual sorting still has a place, time consuming though it is. To rub one's nose in the data helps the interpretation of results and acts as a check against the absurd error which a machine can make, but a man can hardly fail to see. Some of the best insights come during the more tedious routines of research when one has the feel of the data.

## SUMMARY

Data processing condenses raw data into tables of results on which statistical analyses can be performed. The following methods are commonly used: ledger method; written cards; hand-sorted punched cards; mechanically-sorted punched cards; computer input punched cards. The ledger method is inflexible and hence rarely used, except for listing code numbers and names. For samples of up to about 250, written cards are the simplest. Hand-sorted punched cards are suitable for storing data from samples of up to about 1,000, if no more than fifteen to twenty variables have been included. Mechanically-sorted punched cards enable the research worker to follow the sorting process and make immediate checks on puzzling results. Where a large number of interrelations are being investigated, the computer provides the best solution to data-processing problems. The print-out from the computer contains tables of results and tests of statistical significance on those results.

The following processes are involved in transforming raw data into tabular form through the sorting of punched cards:

1. A coding scheme for translating scores into coded categories.
2. A coding sheet for each individual containing his coded scores.
3. A punched card from each coding sheet.
4. *Either* a sorting schedule specifying the most economical order for the sorts *or* a specification to the computer program interpreting the variables and containing instructions as to which tables are to be formed.

## CHAPTER 7

Environmental Factors

An important topic in educational research in recent years has been the influence of environmental factors on children's progress in school and on their general mental development. 'Environment' is a vague term, sometimes referring specifically to the influence of home, parents and family, and sometimes more generally to sub-cultures or patterns of behaviour and expectation in different social groups or classes. Techniques for collecting information on this aspect are therefore of special importance, but they involve both practical difficulties and problems of classification. Relevant information is obtained either by interview or by questionnaire; so the topic provides an illustration of the rules and cautions listed in chapters 4 and 5. In this chapter the main questions are: what information is relevant, how should it be obtained, and how should it be classified for use in educational research?

Early studies were concerned mainly with the nature–nurture controversy, and were limited to showing that children's performance in tests and in school work was not just a matter of inherited ability but was influenced by environmental factors. The Ministry of Education report, *Early Leaving* (1954), marks an important step forward, for it showed clearly that social factors were associated with the decision of many able children to leave school before completing the courses which their teachers thought them capable of completing. Five years later, in *Home Environment and the School*, Fraser (1959) wrote:

'In spite of general acknowledgement that environmental factors exert considerable influence on a child's school progress, relatively little scientific research has been carried out to determine which aspects of the environment are most influential and which are relatively unimportant' (p. 1).

The focus of interest in this area of research since then has shifted away from merely demonstrating that children from poor homes do in fact suffer handicap towards identifying the environmental factors which affect educational progress. It is not sufficient to show that social class affects educational opportunity; we must know how social factors operate if we are to begin to tackle the problem. There has also been a shift away from emphasis on a single global measure of social class towards interest in the specific environmental variables lying behind social class. This tendency is illustrated by the studies summarized by Wiseman (1964, chapter 4) in *Education and Environment*, and also in the research papers, some theoretical and some experimental, brought together by Halsey, Floud and Anderson (1961) in *Education, Economy and Society*. The Plowden Report (Department of Education and Science, 1967) also contains a discussion on social variables related to the reading attainment of children in primary schools.

While this trend towards measurement of individual social variables is continuing, for many purposes it is still useful to obtain a single over-all indication of social class or socio-economic status.

SOCIAL CLASS

The social class to which children belong is usually measured by classifying father's occupation on the Registrar-General's Scale. Father's occupation has been widely used as an indication of social class for a number of reasons. It can be recorded on a form or reported by a child, without the hostility which may be generated by more personal questions; and it affords a tolerably adequate basis for grading of home background, providing that one is dealing with averages from large groups and not with individual cases. Even so, if this information is sought from the schoolchildren themselves, two important precautions must be observed. First, it is necessary to make sure that there is no objection either from teachers or parents to such questions being asked. As the public becomes educated to understand the importance of research into social factors, one would hope that these objections would be less frequent; but there is still a residue of suspicion on such matters. Questioning must always take account of quite proper sensitivity to probing into personal matters: thus, it is important to provide a safeguard for the illegitimate child (see item 2, p. 68). Secondly, the children will require assistance from teachers to ensure that the information is accurate and can be classified. Most children aged ten or eleven can give fairly precise details of their fathers' occupations, but some are wildly inaccurate.

If the information on father's occupation is to be correct, it requires something more than an informal question. For schoolchildren, the teacher's assistance is needed, and the teacher must be given detailed guidance. For adults, especially those with limited education, an interview may be necessary. A simple question on a form, asking for a statement of occupation, will yield unclassifiable replies such as 'factory worker', 'supervisor', 'sailor', 'civil servant', 'engineer', 'police', 'railways', 'shop', or 'office'. These may refer to jobs ranging from the professional to semi-skilled. How does one classify 'retired' or 'unemployed'?

An example is given below of the instructions given to teachers in an Aberdeen study in which children aged ten and eleven were asked for information on father's occupation. These instructions are set out as an illustration rather than as a model. In other areas, different examples will be more appropriate, and other points may require to be made. The notes for guidance set out here are far from adequate; but if too much detail is given or too many complications are described, the result may defeat the purpose as people will not trouble to read it all. Pupils entered on a form their answers to two questions: What is your father's job? Where does he work? (This second question is helpful only for a research confined to one region where the research workers are sufficiently familiar with local industry to make use of the answers given. Otherwise an alternative question might be: What sort of work does he do in this job?)

ANSWERING QUESTIONS ON FATHER'S OCCUPATION

*Guidance for teachers*

*What is your father's job?* Pupils may need assistance in giving this information. Tell the pupils, if they are not sure what to write, to put their hands up.

*Where does he work?* The name of the firm will do here. If the father is not employed by any firm but works on his own (e.g. has his own shop), or if he holds a professional appointment (e.g. a doctor in general practice), the pupil may leave this line blank. The purpose of this question is to enable the father's occupation to be classified more precisely.

In cases of doubt, as much information as possible should be given. The following notes may provide guidance in difficult cases.

1. If the father is *out of work, retired or dead*, the usual or former occupation should be given.
2. Where it is not possible for the pupil to state the father's occupation, the pupil may write 'not known', to avoid any embarrassment. Where pupils are merely uncertain what to write, the teacher will often be able to help in making the correct entry.
3. If the occupation is concerned with *trade or manufacture*, the particular kind of work or the material or article worked should be given, if possible; e.g. not just 'factory worker', but 'foreman in a sausage factory'; not just 'shop-keeper', but 'grocer (own shop)' or 'shop assistant in a chemist's'. Where pupils are not precise, please ask them for further information.
4. Where the father has more than one paid occupation, the occupation given should be that by which mainly he earns (or earned) his living (e.g. a retired policeman employed as a night watchman is 'police constable, retired').

There remains a further problem—how to classify the information on occupations. Various scales are available. The most useful source book is *Classification of Occupations*, 1960 (Registrar-

General, 1960). This provides a comprehensive list of occupations in Britain and explains the procedure for classifying under one of the five headings of the Registrar-General's Scale:

   I Professional and managerial occupations
   II Intermediate occupations
   III Skilled occupations
   IV Partly skilled occupations
   V Unskilled occupations

Social class III in this scale is by far the largest section of the population, and does not distinguish between certain non-manual or clerical occupations and manual occupations, a distinction which is important if a small sample has to be divided into only two categories, manual and non-manual. For relatively small-scale studies with samples of up to 1,000 a convenient form of classification divides social class III into manual and non-manual parts and groups I and II together.

## I/II *Professional and managerial*

Accountants; actuaries; accounting, costing, pay and bank clerks; architects; army, navy and air force officers; civil servants (administrative and executive grade), officers of local authorities; clergymen; doctors; engineers (with degree qualifications); farmers; lawyers; managers; nurses; pharmacists; police inspectors; shop proprietors and managers; surveyors; teachers.

## III *Non-manual: clerical and non-manual skilled*

Clerks (including civil service and local government clerical grades); assistant nurses, medical auxiliaries; commercial travellers; hairdressers; policemen; post office sorters, telegraphists and supervisors; secretaries (not company secretaries), shorthand typists and office machine operators; shop assistants.

## III *Manual: skilled manual*

Builders, masons, plasterers, slaters, carpenters, joiners, plumbers, painters, electricians, fitters, mechanics, machine erectors, radio mechanics, platers, riveters, metalworkers, instrument makers, bus and lorry drivers, roundsmen and van drivers; printers; engine drivers, skilled railway workers; skilled agricultural workers; tailors; H. M. Forces (other ranks); trawler skippers.

## IV *Semi-skilled*

Agricultural workers; barmen; bus conductors; foundry labourers; garment machinists; laundry workers; packers, oilers and greasers; railway firemen; fishermen.

## V *Unskilled*

Dock labourers, navvies, porters; lift attendants; costermongers, hawkers, newspaper sellers; watchmen; kitchen hands.

Various research investigations have devised their own systems of classification, and their reports set out in full the systems they have used: see, for example, pp. 70–6 of *Social Implications of the 1947 Scottish Mental Survey* (Scottish Council for Research in Education, 1953), or chapter 2 of D. V. Glass' (1954) *Social Mobility in Britain*. The form of classification used depends on the size of the sample and especially on the purpose of the research. A sound rule for all except the most experienced of social research worker is to follow a standard system, usually the Registrar-General's Scale. If a new system of classification is used in an investigation, the results cannot readily be related to those of other studies; and since an understanding of social problems must be built up gradually from a whole range of related studies, each sketching in some part of the over-all pattern, a private system of classification will prevent a study from receiving the attention it may deserve.

### FAMILY SIZE AND POSITION IN FAMILY

Occupation is the most effective single measure of social differences in the family environment, but it is a crude global measure, and an indirect one. More direct measures are possible, though the relevance of much of this information to educational progress and personal development is still far from clear. As examples, family size and position in family are direct indices of one aspect of the family environment, but again many children cannot provide this information correctly. In one study an age-group of eleven-year-old children were asked to state how many brothers and sisters they had. Individual interviews of a random sample of 200 of these revealed errors in 10 per cent of the original answers— omission of grown-up siblings who had left home, inclusion of cousins who shared the home, or even simple errors of arithmetic (Nisbet, 1953, appendix B; see also Roberts, 1939). Again a more elaborate procedure is necessary to help children to give accurate replies. Ask the child to write down the names of *older* brothers and sisters, including any who are grown up and have left home; and then to write down the names of *younger* brothers and sisters. Position and size are then recorded as 1/3 (oldest of three), 2/4 (second in a family of four), 1/1 (only child) and so on. Twins are recorded as both having the senior position (1T/2 for both twins in a family of two), but they may have to be excluded, or treated separately, in an analysis involving family size and position.

Additional direct measures of family environment which may readily be included on an interview schedule are type of house, number of rooms in the house or parents' education. Other direct measures, such as possession of a car or telephone, may only be effective within defined regions or groups and their meaning may change in a relatively short span of years.

SOCIAL AND CULTURAL LEVEL OF THE HOME

Fraser's survey of previous investigations (1959, chapter 2) includes an interesting account of attempts to measure home background as they have been developed over the past fifty years. Ideally, one might hope to find one single measure, such as the income of the father, which would give an accurate indication of the social and cultural level of the home. But there are two immediate objections to using this obvious measure: first, the information is difficult to obtain, since this is not a matter on which people in Britain speak freely to strangers; and secondly, it is not enough by itself, since it is often more important to know how the money is used rather than how much of it there is. Consequently, the early studies sought to construct a socio-economic index developed from a differential weighting of various objectively assessed features of home background. This approach can perhaps best be understood by the analogy of a cost-of-living index, which is based on prices of selected items chosen as a representative sample of all the many items which make up the total cost of living. Thus the Whittier Scale for Grading Home Conditions (Williams, 1916) comprised five assessments of the home: provision of necessities; neatness; size; parental conditions; and parental supervision. Each aspect was assessed on a five-point scale by an interviewer who visited the home, and the score on the scale was the sum of the five ratings.

Fraser's own study is one of the most detailed studies of the various aspects of home background. She classified these under four main headings:

'*a*) *Cultural*. Information in this category concerns such factors as the educational level of the parents, the books in the home, the reading habits of the parents, and their leisure interests.

*b*) *Material and economic*. Into this category fall data on income of parents and of siblings, and general living conditions as measured by the number of rooms in the home in relation to the number of persons sharing them.

*c*) *Motivational*. In this category the relevant items are those concerned with the parents' attitudes towards the child's educational progress and future employment, and the encouragement the parents give him in his school work.

*d*) *Emotional*. In this category the relevant information comprises the degree of harmony in the home, the emotional security of the child, and the interest taken by the parents in the child's general welfare.'

Under each heading specific items were assessed. Each item was objectively defined on a scale; and points were awarded arbitrarily to each step on each scale, to enable the evidence derived from a visit to the home to be added together in a comprehensive index of home environment. The list of items assessed was:

| | | |
|---|---|---|
| '*a*) *Cultural* | 1 | Parents' education |
| | 2 | Reading habits of parents and children |
| *b*) *Material* | 3 | Income |
| | 4 | Occupation of father |
| | 5 | Family size |
| | 6 | Living space |
| *c*) *Motivational* | 7 | Parents' attitudes to the education and future employment of the child |
| | 8 | Parental encouragement |
| *d*) *Emotional* | 9 | Abnormal home background |
| | 10 | General impression of the home background |
| | 11 | Mother out at work' |

For item 1, the parents' education, points were awarded on the basis of (*a*) the duration of any course of education after age of fourteen; (*b*) qualifications resulting from it; and (*c*) the academic standard required by the course. For item 2, reading habits, the aspects assessed covered library membership, number of books in the home, frequency and quality of reading, daily newspapers read, and Sunday papers and magazines read. A full account is given in chapter 5 of Fraser's book.

The development of similar scales of parental attitudes is reported in the Plowden Report (volume 2, appendix 3). These scales were derived from a factor analysis of the questions on the interview schedule already described in chapter 4 of this book. Further analysis in the Plowden Report showed a relation between parents' attitudes and children's scores on a reading test. In evaluating the value of these results or those from similar studies it is important to realize that the scales are far from objective and also that the relations may not be causal. The results are always influenced by the particular questions asked and the way in which the data have been collected. Furthermore, a close relation between any one aspect of environment and children's success in school must not be interpreted as evidence of causal link. Thus parents' membership of a library may be related to children's attainment; but library membership is an indirect measure of educational or cultural level, and so may be merely an objective (and not particularly accurate) means of identifying much more general differences between families. All the various measures tend to be correlated with each other, and the general factor which accounts for this overlapping must be similar to what is commonly referred to as social class.

DEMOGRAPHIC VARIABLES

A different approach to the measurement of home background is the demographic method, illustrated by Wiseman's *Education and Environment* (1964), or by his study (1967) reported in appendix 9 in volume 2 of the Plowden Report. A much earlier study by Burt (1937) in chapter 5 of *The Backward Child* also uses similar indices of environment, which are based on the community, rather than the individual family, as a unit of measurement. The variables are the statistics of delinquency, free meals, incidence of illness, housing, school attendance, and so on. These are 'hard' or exact statistics which justify more sophisticated techniques of statistical analysis. Wiseman (1964) reports a factor analysis of social variables together with measures of attainment. The demographic variables were taken from different parts of Manchester and district; educational attainment was based on the standards reached in schools in the same areas. The whole analysis showed that demographic variables are related to attainment, but they have less direct relevance to the educational problems of individual families. The demographic approach is at the opposite extreme to the interview method used by Fraser and described earlier in this chapter, where the data are more difficult to quantify but are more obviously relevant.

In assessing environmental factors the research worker often has to choose between the objectivity of either direct measures of home background and demographic variables and the educational relevance of the more subjective assessments of parents' attitudes. As one moves towards the kind of measurement which is likely to be most directly relevant to children's progress in school, the measures become less objective, less precise and more difficult to assess. In many studies this problem is side-stepped by including a combination of both direct and indirect measures in the survey.

SUMMARY

The environmental factor most commonly measured in relation to children's school progress is social class. Father's occupation graded by the Registrar-General's Scale provides a basis for assessing a child's social class, but recent research has concentrated on more precise indications of the factors related to educational achievement. Family size, position in family, size of house and parents' education, all provide direct measures of home environment; but these are rarely found to be closely related to either intelligence or attainment. Parental attitudes and other indications of the social and cultural level of the home are more difficult to assess, but have more obvious relevance to children's behaviour in school. Fraser (1959) and the Plowden Report (1967) both report scales measuring specific aspects of home background. The demographic approach to measuring environmental factors makes use of community variables, as opposed to measures of the home background of individual families. The 'hard' statistics of juvenile delinquency and incidence of various illnesses in geographical areas justify sophisticated statistical methods, but show only weak relations with educational attainment.

| Abilities and Attainments

The measurement of abilities and attainments is the area in which educational research has made most progress towards a systematic theory. Many of the important investigations date from before 1950, when it was customary to make a clear distinction between ability and attainment. A common assumption was that ability 'caused' attainment, or that tests of attainment indicated how far potential ability has been realized. The intelligence test was sometimes used as if it were a measure of this potential ability. Tests of aptitude formed a third category, being measures of special ability, or of potential for skill in a specialized area of performance. Ability, aptitude and attainment are no longer accepted as representing separate psychological dimensions; they are inter-related and so overlap each other.

As early as 1955, Vernon put forward this view:

'I know that psychologists have usually postulated a clear distinction between intelligence ... and acquired information .... I would say that a relative distinction may still be useful between the more general qualities of comprehending, judging, reasoning and efficiency of thinking ... and such skills and knowledge as are specifically taught. ... But I do not accept the formulation that intelligence ... causes or makes possible the acquisition of attainments. One might equally say that the attainments cause the intelligence' (pp. 10–11).

A full discussion of this point, and of the nature of abilities, is to be found in Vernon's *Intelligence and Attainment Tests* (1960) or, more recently, in Butcher's *Human Intelligence* (1968). While there should be no assumption of psychological reality in divisions between ability, aptitude and attainment, these categories continue to be used when referring to measurement techniques.

This book does not offer any detailed description of published tests. The emphasis is on how to use these tests in educational research. There is a good choice of well-written textbooks on the subject of psychological and educational measurement, some covering the general field (including personality measurement) and others more specifically concerned with educational or statistical aspects:

ANASTASI, A. (1961) *Psychological Testing* (New York: Macmillan)

ANSTEY, E. (1966) *Psychological Tests* (London: Nelson)

CRONBACH, L. J. (1964*a*) *Essentials of Psychological Testing* (New York: Harper)

NUNNALLY, J. C. (1967) *Psychometric Theory* (New York: McGraw-Hill)

PIDGEON, D. and YATES, A. (1968) *An Introduction to Educational Measurement* (London: Routledge & Kegan Paul)

## USE OF STANDARDIZED TESTS

This chapter is concerned with *standardized* tests: school examinations and teachers' marks are dealt with in chapter 9. Where it is possible to choose between using a standardized test in research and making up one's own test, the advantage obviously lies with the standardized test. It is economical to take advantage of the work of others in preparing an accurate and discriminating instrument; the standardized test is likely to be much more reliable (and probably more valid) than a home-made version; and research which is based on nationally available material can more readily be assessed and replicated.

The most detailed catalogue of tests is the *Mental Measurements Yearbook*, an authoritative reference text of which six volumes have now been produced by its editor, O. K. Buros. The Sixth Yearbook (1965) contains 1,714 pages, of which 123 are index. In addition to a factual description of the tests listed, there are two commentaries on each test by educational and psychological authorities, who pick out the merits and defects and discuss the use of the test. A short version, *Tests in Print* (1965), lists only the factual information on the tests. A detailed account of tests currently available and commonly used in Britain is to be found in Stephen Jackson's *A Teacher's Guide to Tests and Testing* (1969).

The test catalogues of the National Foundation for Educational Research, of the Psychological Corporation, New York, and of educational publishers, should also be consulted. However, the fact that a test is published by a reputable firm is no guarantee of its value. Many out-dated tests are still advertised and sold, either because stocks have to be cleared or because a demand is created by unwary users.

Most texts on educational or psychological measurement tend to concentrate on the statistical aspects. Here we are more concerned with other important considerations in the choice and use of tests, which are seriously neglected in most statistical texts. How, for example, does one decide whether a test is suitable for a particular use? To judge a test, one must look not only at the test itself but also, and perhaps more important, at the test manual. The manual should give details of how the test was constructed and the age-range of the sample used for standardization; it should state the reliability coefficient and report briefly the evidence of validity, in the form of correlations with other tests, with teachers' ratings, or with subsequent performance. The different types of validity are mentioned in the appendix to this chapter.

Before any test is used, it is necessary to check various technical details in the test manual. Some rule-of-thumb principles can be stated as a guide. A test of ability or attainment which has a reliability coefficient of less than $+0.90$ should not be used. Test norms are suspect unless they are derived from a representative sample of at least 1,000 cases. If the test has been standardized on a sample which is not representative of the group to which the test is to be applied, or, as is too often the case, if no details of the standardization are given in the manual, the test must be used with great caution and the results interpreted with care.

Simple rules like these, however, are not an adequate substitute for an understanding of the techniques of test construction, which is essential for a proper judgement to be made on a test. A non-statistical treatment of test construction and item analysis is given in the appendix to this chapter: a detailed account can be found in the books by Anstey (1966) or Nunnally (1967).

In choosing a test for a research project, a major consideration is the age-range for which the test is suited. However satisfactory the reliability and validity statistics in the manual, these do not apply if the test is used with children of an age-range for which the test is not suited. If the children are too young, the test may become a measure of perseverance or self-confidence—how quickly they give up or become disheartened—or whether some are prepared to guess blindly and so run up a modest score by chance alone, while the painstaking scholar may fail even to get a chance score because he hesitates to be wrong. If the test is too easy, it may measure only speed of working, or the meticulous kind of accuracy which gains 98 right out of 100 against the 90 of a more able child who is impatient of easy questions. (Accuracy is, of course, a virtue, but it is a source of contamination if we are trying to assess non-verbal reasoning with a timed test.) Between ages 8 and 10 a difficult printed test often becomes a test of reading ability. Whatever the test is called—verbal reasoning, problem arithmetic, creativity—successful performance on it depends on ability to understand the printed instructions. This important fact is often overlooked when the results from such tests are interpreted.

These points illustrate the danger of an unintelligent use of standardized tests. Other snags are out-of-date or inappropriate norms or unfamiliar terminology or lay-out. Norms provide the basis for the conversion tables, which show whether a score is above or below average for a given age: they are derived from the standardization in which the test was given to a representative sample of a given age-range, and the scores of this sample determine what is an average performance. Attainment in reading and certain arithmetic processes is at a higher standard than twenty years ago: thus a twenty-year-old test is more flattering than an up-to-date one. Certain processes are no longer taught in school, and certain ways of setting out arithmetic sums are unfamiliar to pupils who have been brought up on 'new' maths: parts of an old-style test may be unintelligible to present-day pupils. Obviously, American tests may require some translation of words like 'tardy' or modification of unfamiliar material; less obviously, norms can be misleading, especially at age 6, 7, and 8 and in secondary school tests. American children start school a year later than British children, and generally have lower attainment standards in the early stages of primary school, though they catch up by age 10 or 11. The secondary school curriculum tends to be organized differently in American schools, and standards are not comparable with those of British schools. Even within Britain, geographical differences cannot be ignored: testing of Hebridean children, for example, must take account of the fact that few children have seen a train and that umbrellas are unfamiliar in a climate where strong winds are more frequent than in London. (Trains and umbrellas are mentioned in items in the widely used Stanford-Binet Scale of Intelligence.)

These are minor points: a more general point is that, in evaluating the results of an experiment, the research worker cannot be sure of objectivity or lack of bias merely by choosing a published 'objective' test. An experimental programme is expected to end with a different product from a conventional programme, and one cannot always evaluate that product by conventional measures. The choice of test can bias results if the content of the test favours one treatment more than the others. This problem bedevils attempts at evaluation in curriculum development projects, as we shall see in chapter 14. The choice of the 'right' measure of attainment is crucial in many studies. A test of word recognition may give different results from a test of comprehension—even though both are called 'reading tests'— when applied in an investigation of methods of teaching reading. The evaluation of i.t.a. provides an example of how difficult it is to choose a truly objective measure (see Downing, 1967).

The discussion in the last few pages has centred on the general principles of choosing a suitable standardized test. The next sections comment briefly on the varieties of tests of ability, aptitude and attainment which have been published.

## TESTS OF ABILITY

Bearing in mind the warning given at the beginning of this chapter, it is important to realize that there is no such thing as a test of 'pure' intelligence or general ability. Scores on any test of 'intelligence' will be influenced by extraneous factors such as previous educational experience, home environment and personality factors. On the other hand, it is still useful to have tests which are not related to specific syllabuses, in which the content will be novel to all those taking the test.

Intelligence tests were among the first standardized tests to be devised in the early years of this century. The first was an *individual test* used by Binet to identify mentally deficient children. In an individual test the psychologist takes the child through a series of intellectual problems, some involving word recognition and others relying on the manipulation of cardboard shapes or wooden blocks (*performance tests*). The problems are graded for increasing levels of difficulty and the mental age of the child is measured in terms of the number of problems correctly solved. Originally the intelligence quotient was derived by dividing mental age by chronological age and multiplying this quotient by 100. More recent tests use a statistical technique to introduce age allowances and produce scales with mean scores of 100 and standard deviations of approximately 15.

A more recent revision of the Binet scale is the Stanford-Binet in which the majority of sub-scales have a strong verbal bias. The Weschler tests for adults and children provide both verbal and non-verbal sub-scores. The new British Intelligence Scale (Warburton, 1966) is of a similar design. While these individual tests of ability are widely used in clinics for determining degrees of intellectual subnormality, they may take one hour or more to administer. In educational research *group tests* under examination conditions provide useful, though less accurate, measures of ability. Group tests of verbal or non-verbal reasoning ability generally take about forty-five minutes. Examples of the type of question asked can be found in most of the texts mentioned earlier in the chapter. Verbal reasoning tests have been used extensively in 11-plus selection procedures throughout Britain. The majority of these tests were devised either by the Godfrey Thomson Unit for Educational Research (Moray House tests) or by the National Foundation for Educational Research. To ensure that the contents of these tests were kept secret, the tests have been made available only to local authorities or research workers (*closed tests*). Similar tests or older ones not used for selection purposes are available from the NFER and from other publishers (*open tests*). Psychological tests which require skilled administration or interpretation are also restricted; they are issued only to people with appropriate educational or psychological qualifications.

TESTS OF APTITUDE

Intelligence tests are designed to estimate general ability and show high correlations with measures of over-all school attainment. They may produce rather poor estimates of performance in particular subjects. Aptitude tests are measures of narrow areas of ability and are often used to indicate whether a person has special skills necessary for a particular job or for a specific course of study.

The use of tests for guidance and counselling, both academic and vocational, is an area in which research is urgently needed. At first sight, there appears to be quite a good variety of aptitude tests available—mechanical aptitude, musical ability, clerical and stenographic tests, and so on. The present tendency is to develop batteries of tests, such as the Differential Aptitude Test Battery (Bennett, Seashore and Wesman, 1966). A pupil's scores in the whole battery give a 'profile' which indicates his strengths and weaknesses. One danger of relying too much on such a 'profile' is that the amount of chance error in a difference between two scores is greater than the error in any one score. The profile may reflect only these chance errors or may simply serve to indicate that there are differences in the validity and reliability of the various tests making up the battery. This is particularly liable to happen if the tests are relatively short; reliability is affected by test length.

A more serious problem in the use of aptitude tests can best be explained by a specific illustration (Kirkwood, 1962). The Modern Language Aptitude Test (Carroll and Sapon, 1955) was given to a group of Aberdeen children starting to learn French. The experimental design was the standard validation procedure for aptitude tests which are used for predicting later attainment: performance on this aptitude test was compared with examination results at the end of the first year of learning French. The test was reasonably successful in forecasting those who had difficulty in learning French, or, at least, those who failed to learn from this particular method of teaching. Is the next step, then, to use this aptitude test to prevent pupils with low scores embarking on the course, so as to avoid wasting the teacher's time and energy and to protect the pupils from the discouragement of failure? Or should the results of the validation be used as a stimulus to the teacher to discover a different method of teaching from which these pupils *can* benefit? The point of this illustration is that tests do not always answer questions for us; if they are properly used, on the other hand, they may sharpen our thinking by directing attention to the relevant questions.

## TESTS OF ATTAINMENT

Tests which are specifically related to syllabuses, as tests of attainment must be, have a limited range of usefulness, and many of those which are available are far from being entirely satisfactory. Though there is a good range of tests of reading, vocabulary, language usage, spelling and various arithmetical skills, there are few tests suitable for other aspects of the primary school curriculum. The teacher may argue that it is inappropriate to use standardized tests for assessing work in parts of the curriculum not mainly concerned with teaching skills. This objection certainly applies to testing as a regular part of the school programme; but a research study on attainments in the modern primary school would have limited usefulness if it was restricted to an evaluation of skills. At the secondary school level it is difficult to find any attainment tests suitable for use in Britain. Certain NFER tests and Percival's tests of French vocabulary and grammar (1963) are among the few available. American publishers have produced batteries of attainment tests covering a wide range of the curriculum, but the content is often inappropriate to British syllabuses. As a standardized test of attainment can be developed only for a standard syllabus, it is impossible to find tests which are wholly appropriate for non-traditional syllabuses. The implications for curriculum development work have already been mentioned. Faced with a lack of suitable standardized tests a research team must devise its own evaluation instruments, by methods such as those described in chapter 9. Alternatively, a procedure for moderating school assessments, such as is used in CSE Mode 3 examinations, may be used; this also is described in chapter 9.

DIAGNOSTIC TESTS

Attainment is measured in terms of the number of correct answers made by a pupil; diagnostic tests are used to identify and to categorize the types of *mistakes* made by the pupil. In this way the weak points in his learning may be diagnosed and these weaknesses remedied. Research workers have tended to ignore the uses of diagnostic tests, although an important approach towards understanding how pupils learn can be made through analysing the errors they make. Attainment tests can be used diagnostically, but they are not designed specifically for this purpose. The scores of children on an attainment test should be well spread out, with only a comparatively small number of high scores. The distribution of scores from a diagnostic test is quite different. Most pupils should have all or nearly all items correct, as diagnostic tests are usually used to investigate the different types of errors made by the weaker pupils. Some pupils tend to make mistakes of one type more than another, and the type of error made indicates the nature of remedial teaching which is required.

For example, spelling errors may be classified as follows (the list is a version of one developed by Burt, 1922, adapted to include suggestions by Schonell, 1942):

1. *Lapses*
   The child knows the correct spelling but fails to reproduce it. If the test is repeated, the error does not recur.
2. *Extemporizations*
   The child invents a spelling. If the test is repeated, the error appears again with a different spelling.
3. *Habitual errors*
   The child has learnt an incorrect form. The same error is always repeated.
4. *Diagnostic signs*
   a) Weak visual memory, auditory substitution: kwickly, boutyfol.
   b) Weak auditory analysis: slool (school), chardren (children), Moday (Monday).
   c) Reversals, weak left–right sequence: gril (girl), agian (again), no (on), dig (big).

A more detailed discussion of diagnostic signs is to be found in Schonell (1942).

Since arithmetic involves a hierarchical structure of skills, the more complex procedures being developed on the basis of simple skills, the diagnostic approach is particularly appropriate. Schonell's Diagnostic Arithmetic Test comprises twelve sub-tests, each of which is directed to one aspect of arithmetic. Sub-test 1 (Addition), for example, lists the hundred combinations of the digits 0 to 9: by the age of eight most pupils will add these correctly, but from the errors made the teacher can identify the number combinations which cause a pupil difficulty—such as combinations involving a zero, $7 + 0 = ?$ Sub-test 6 has groups of four items for each stage in the addition process: the first four are straightforward addition of small numbers; the second four introduce zeros; the next group involve larger numbers; and the fourth larger still. Then carrying is introduced with progressively larger numbers, and so on.

Similar tests have been devised for reading—for example, lists of words which are particularly susceptible to reversal, like 'was', 'saw', 'who', 'how', 'top', 'bad' (see Schonell, 1942, chapter 8).

A detailed account of diagnostic testing procedures would have to include other more complex psychological tests, such as the Bender Gestalt Test or the Frostig Developmental Test of Visual Perception. Many of these are still at the development stage, and the techniques of application and interpretation belong to the field of clinical procedures, rather than to that of research methods.

## DEVELOPMENT OF CHILDREN'S THINKING

Another form of test which deserves mention is that which assesses the *stage of development* which a child has reached, instead of attempting to produce scores by which children can be ranked in order of merit. These tests are based on the stages outlined by Piaget: for example, they test whether or not a child has grasped the concept of conservation of weight or of volume. Discussion of these tests would go beyond the scope of this chapter; they are mentioned here to show that abilities and attainments should not be regarded solely as involving quantitative measurement. The analysis of qualitative differences in children's thinking is an important and rapidly developing area of research. The study of *how* children reason in answering test problems (Donaldson, 1963) is referred to in chapter 13, where individual case studies are considered. Tests of creativity (chapter 10) provide another example of how research on abilities has extended far beyond the narrow concept of measurement associated with the early days of intelligence and attainment tests.

## SUMMARY

Ability, aptitude and attainment are not distinct psychological dimensions. Tests designed to measure one of these will also measure components of the others. Before choosing a standardized test it is important to check the details given in the manual about reliability and validity. The sizes and age-ranges of the samples used for standardization of the test are also important. Always use a test specifically designed for the age-group and nationality of children from which the sample is to be drawn. If this is not possible, the results must be treated with great caution.

Ability tests are often divided into individual or group tests and into verbal or non-verbal, depending on their content and method of application. Although certain 'open' tests are available from publishers, many tests have restrictions placed on their use. Aptitude tests are used to measure specific areas of ability so as to predict likely success in either a future job or a course of study. But profiles of scores derived from a differential aptitude battery can be misleading, because of chance differences between scores in the sub-tests.

As attainment tests have to be related to specific syllabuses, many published scales are unsuitable for modern curricula. The norms of tests based on children from other countries are unlikely to be appropriate for British children. Diagnostic tests aim at identifying the particular types of mistakes made by pupils so that these weaknesses may be remedied. The stage of mental development reached by a child may be measured by tests of concept formation such as those used by Piaget. Both diagnostic tests and measures of concept development assess qualitative differences between individuals; most standardized tests estimate the over-all level reached in a particular attribute.


APPENDIX ON TEST CONSTRUCTION

The basic principle of test construction is to use careful preliminary trials. The questions (or items) are tested initially in a pilot run, on a sample from the appropriate population. Double the number of items eventually to be used are included in this trial run, since only the best will be retained. The 'best' items are those which are shown to be measuring the same attribute, to be at the right level of difficulty and to discriminate effectively between those with high ability in the quality measured and those with little ability. Each of these points requires elaboration.

First 'measuring the same attribute'. If we are intending to measure verbal reasoning, we do not want to include items which depend mainly on reading ability, or arithmetical knowledge. Some of the items which are inappropriate can be detected by inspection, but a precise objective analysis using the data from the pilot run is still necessary. This procedure is known as *item analysis*. In the simplest form of item analysis, the test booklets of the trial sample are divided into three equal piles, the top third on total scores, the middle third, and the third who have the lowest total scores. Performance on each item is then checked, to see how many have the correct answer in each third. The percentages of correct responses made to each item by the different groups are calculated and a table, such as the one below, is built up to summarize the results. If we select only those items where there is a marked difference between the percentage correct in the top third and in the bottom third, with a steady progression through the middle third, we can assume (though with some reservations) that the items are measuring the same ability: they are, at least, working together (are intercorrelated).

| Item no. | Percentage of correct responses | | | Total | Index of discrimination* |
|---|---|---|---|---|---|
| | Top third | Middle third | Bottom third | | |
| 1 | 75 | 55 | 20 | 50 | +55 |
| 2 | 95 | 88 | 81 | 88 | +14 |
| 3 | 48 | 12 | 9 | 23 | +39 |
| 4 | 65 | 58 | 60 | 61 | + 5 |

* Formed by subtracting the percentage correct response of the bottom third from that of the top third

The difference between the percentages in columns 1 and 3 above is an index of the discrimination of the item. It would be impossible to find items answered correctly by all the best pupils and by none of the worst pupils. Usually a discrimination level of 30 per cent is taken as justifying inclusion and, on this basis, *item 1* is excellent. It is also at the right level of difficulty, as half the sample have answered it correctly. On the other hand, item 2 is too easy and should be omitted. An item which everyone or no one answered correctly can contribute nothing to discriminating between good and poor performances and is therefore wasted. A certain number of easy items may be used to provide a gentle introduction to a test, but the usual rule is that items answered by more than 80 per cent or less than 20 per cent are dropped. Item 3 discriminates well at the upper levels of ability, but is near the limit of difficulty: not too many items as hard as this should be included. Item 4 does not discriminate effectively and should be omitted.

There is common fallacy that a good test always produces a normal distribution of raw scores (that is, of the actual totals of items correct). The distribution of scores in a test depends on the difficulty of the items selected, and there is no special merit in ensuring that these follow the normal curve. It is always possible to impose a normal distribution subsequently by use of a conversion table which changes raw scores into quotients. The distribution of raw scores should be deliberately planned to suit the purpose of the test. If the test is intended to discriminate among the ablest pupils only, the distribution should be positively skewed: that is, there is an accumulation of low scores, but the higher scores are spaced out over a wider range. Conversely, a test which is aimed at distinguishing the weakest pupils (such as a diagnostic test) and which is not concerned with differences between 'above average' and 'outstanding' pupils will have a negatively skewed distribution, with an accumulation of scores at the 'ceiling' of the test (that is, near the maximum total). A test which is designed to discriminate at all levels of ability should have a rectangular distribution, with approximately the same proportion of pupils scoring at each level of score.

Although item analysis by hand is a laborious procedure, it can be done rapidly by computer. There are also various short-cut methods (see Connaughton and Skurnik, 1969), and modifications of the method described above: for example, there is a good statistical reason for preferring a cut-off of the top and bottom 27 per cent or 25 per cent instead of the top and bottom third.

The *reliability* of a test indicates how consistently it measures— that is, whether it gives the same or nearly the same score when it is administered a second time. This is expressed as a correlation coefficient: the reliability should be between 0·90 and 0·96. It can be calculated by a test re-test procedure, in which scores obtained on the two occasions are intercorrelated. Alternatively it can be estimated by the split-half method, in which the score on the odd-numbered items is set against the score on the even-numbered items. The coefficient obtained by the split-half method should be corrected for the effect of reduced length, unless it is a timed or speed test. Reliability can also be calculated by various formulae from the item-analysis data (such as the Kuder-Richardson formulae).

The *validity* of a test is a measure of how well it tests what it is intended to test. The first point to note is that a test cannot be valid unless it has high reliability. A test producing inconsistent scores cannot be valid, but on the other hand it may have reliability without being valid: consistency is no guarantee that the test has measured what was intended. There are also different types of validity which are established using different procedures.

*Predictive validity* is assessed by a follow-up, to see if test scores predict performance in a course or on a job. *Concurrent validity* is the agreement of the test with other valid measures of the same attribute taken at the same time. *Construct validity* is demonstrated when the scores on a test of some carefully defined attribute (construct) are shown to correspond to known or genuine differences in the samples being used. For example, construct validity may be inferred if scores on an anxiety test are shown to rise when the subjects are put under stress. *Content validity* (or face validity) refers to the apparent appropriateness of the test material to what is being measured.

In addition to these technical aspects, the points already mentioned should be observed. A research worker planning to use a test should check the size and composition of the standardization sample, the age-range for which the test is designed, and the date when the test was compiled in case changes of curriculum or standard have made it out of date. It is also advisable to examine the table of norms, to see if the range of variation expected to result from the experiment is one which the test will measure accurately. If the expected range is about fifteen points of score on the norms, and this covered by thirty or forty points of raw score, the test can be used; if fifteen points of score on the norms are represented only by ten or twenty points of raw score (as may happen when a test covering a wide age-range is applied to a single age-group), the test should not be used.

## CHAPTER 9

Examination Marks

The study of examinations is itself a topic of research which regularly attracts publicity when findings emerge to the discredit of established examining procedures. This chapter, however, is not concerned with research on examinations, or the larger issue of the function and place of examinations in relation to the aims of education, but rather with the use of examination marks as research measures in education. The research worker often has to make the best of what is available; and when examination marks are all that is available, he must find a way of controlling their more serious inadequacies. For many types of research project, marks provide readily available assessments which can be got without disrupting school work. Moreover, they usually represent a genuine effort on the part of the pupils, whereas a specially applied test or inventory—especially if it is of an exotic kind— may be treated as a joke or as a bore. Social science students are particularly prone to treat tests in this way, as they are often exposed to a surfeit of such experiences.

RANGE OF MARKS

One major defect of examination marks as measures of perform- ance is that marks from one examination (or from one marker, if the marking of a large batch of papers is shared) are not directly comparable with those from another. The differences between two sets of examination marks may be differences in standard, or differences in range or scatter, or both at once. Differences in standard occur when results from an easy examination are combined with results from a difficult examination, or when one marker is strict and another lenient. Differences in scatter occur when, say, a set of English marks is added to or compared with a set of mathematics marks. Where there is a pass-mark of about 50, the marks in English usually are between 40 and 75 on a percentage scale, but a mathematics examination may result in marks ranging from 20 to 90, or even from 0 to 100.

Such differences are important. At the simplest level, they imply that we cannot tell whether 65 in English is better or worse than 65 in French, or how 60 in one teacher's examination compares with 60 in another's. When marks are added together— for example, to decide class prizes for the year—the mathematics marks generally carry more weight than the English marks in determining the order of merit. This effect is caused by the wide range of marks in most mathematics examinations—a point that can be illustrated by the example shown in table 4. Five pupils take examinations in English, geography and mathematics. The final mark is the sum of the marks in these three subjects.

TABLE 4

EXAMPLE SHOWING EFFECT OF DIFFERENCES IN MARKING
RANGE

| Pupil | maths | Marks in English | geography | Total mark |
|---|---|---|---|---|
| P | 90 | 40 | 20 | 150 |
| Q | 70 | 45 | 30 | 145 |
| R | 50 | 50 | 40 | 140 |
| S | 30 | 55 | 50 | 135 |
| T | 10 | 60 | 60 | 130 |
| Range of marks | 80 | 20 | 40 | |

Although the orders of merit in both English and geography are identical (pupil T being first and pupil P last), the final order is determined by the mathematics examination in which that order is reversed. A similar effect might be found within an examination where marks from different types of question were added together. A geography examination, for example, might consist of three compulsory questions, the first of these being factual (such as a map question) and the remaining questions being answered by essays. The factual question would probably lead to a much wider range of marks than the essay questions. Pupils doing the best maps would then stand a much better chance of obtaining the best marks in the whole examination. The same effect might still be seen in an examination consisting of essay questions marked by different teachers, if the ranges used by these markers were not closely similar. It is generally realized that such markers should agree on their standards, but it is not so well known that their ranges of marks are equally important.

There is also a common idea that the mark assigned to a piece of work indicates the absolute level or standard reached by the pupil. Examination marks provide *essentially* a rank order within the group which has sat the examination. The numbers used to assign marks have no absolute value; they are relative values applicable only within the group. The 10 per cent difference between marks of 70 and 60 may indicate a degree of change in performance quite different from the 10 per cent between 40 and 30. Admittedly, an experienced marker will assign marks with reasonable consistency, so that his 50 per cent for an essay answer means approximately the same standard on each occasion. Differences between markers remain a problem unless the examination is objectively marked (with fixed marks for each correct answer or part of the answer).

Even with this method of marking there is still the difficulty of selecting questions or devising a marking scheme at a level of difficulty which will result in 50 per cent representing approximately the same standard on each occasion. Both of these approaches are open to error, especially with less experienced markers, and the standard set by one person is liable to differ from that set by another. The problem of improving the accuracy of such marking procedures is discussed towards the end of this chapter.

In a standardized test, the raw scores are converted into quotients or percentiles which permit comparisons between tests. This is possible because the tests have been standardized by application to a representative sample in the process of test construction (see chapter 8). But with examination marks, there is no standardization sample to which they can be referred.

There are two main methods of imposing common standards on sets of marks so that they are comparable with each other. In a large national examination like GCE where many markers are used, the Chief Examiner devises a marking scheme, and checks by sampling that the markers are applying it correctly and marking at an appropriate standard. This is an elaborate and costly procedure, applicable only when all the pupils have taken the same examination. It is not often possible to apply this method in equating school examination marks or teachers' estimates, obtained from different classes. It is unusual for all classes, even of the same age, to take the same examination and so the research worker uses a different method of imposing common standards, the method of scaling.

SCALING EXAMINATION MARKS

The basic principle of *scaling* is that a common test has to be given to all the pupils concerned, thus providing a yard-stick against which the performance of each *class* may be compared; within each class the teacher's ratings (or the class examination marks) determine the order of merit. There are various methods by which this can be done. A detailed account is given in McIntosh, Walker and Mackay's (1962) *The Scaling of Teacher's Marks and Estimates*. A summary list of procedures is given in Vernon's (1957) *Secondary School Selection* (appendix D).

The method can be illustrated without statistical complications by describing the form of scaling used in Sweden. (This account is adapted from Henrysson, 1964.)

As part of an attempt to ensure that marks given in a rural school in the north are comparable with marks given in an urban school in the south, Swedish teachers are asked to assess their pupils on a 1 to 7 scale in such a way that fixed percentages of children are put into the different categories, as follows:

| Category | 1 | 2 | 3 | 4 | 5 | 6 | 7 |
|---|---|---|---|---|---|---|---|
| Per cent | 1 | 6 | 24 | 38 | 24 | 6 | 1 |

These percentage distributions are based on national norms of performance. Teachers are asked to bear this distribution in mind when they make their original estimates, but variations from this fixed scheme are allowed. For example, if a class is brighter than average, a teacher may give more high marks; with a homogeneous class, the teacher is allowed to assign the majority of his pupils to a smaller number of categories. But these variations have to be justified by reference to national scales. Standardized tests in key subjects are available throughout Sweden for use by teachers, and raw scores in these tests are converted into the 1 to 7 scale from country-wide norms. To put his own marks on a national scale, a teacher applies one of these tests, calculates the number of his pupils falling into each of the seven categories in that test, and adjusts the distribution of his own marks so that it corresponds approximately to the distribution of marks got by his pupils in the national test. Pupils' order of merit in the final adjusted marks need not agree with the order of merit in the test, but the distribution for the class must agree.

| | | Number of pupils in each category | | |
| | | Teacher's | | Teacher's |
| | | original | Test | adjusted |
| | Category | estimates | scores | estimates |
|---|---|---|---|---|
| Example | 7 | 0 | 1 | 0 |
| from | 6 | 0 | 4 | 4 |
| one | 5 | 4 | 4 | 4 |
| class | 4 | 4 | 9 | 10 |
| | 3 | 14 | 5 | 4 |
| | 2 | 2 | 1 | 2 |
| | 1 | 0 | 0 | 0 |
| No. in class | | 24 | 24 | 24 |

Scaling is particularly useful for adjusting teachers' estimates from a number of schools so that they can be combined in a single set of marks which is fair to pupils in all the schools. A common examination can show whether the general standard of one school is above or below the general standard of another, but it may give inaccurate marks for individual pupils—inaccurate in the sense that the teacher will say of John's mark that it is disappointing, for he usually does better than that, and the teacher is more often right than a single examination mark. A teacher who has worked with a class for a year or more can assign to his pupils estimate marks which, *within his class*, are more accurate than any one test. The obstacle to using these estimates is, of course, that it is difficult to compare the estimates from one teacher with those from another. A test, though inaccurate in individual cases, is much more accurate in measuring the average performance of a group, and the range of performance in the group, for chance errors in individual marks tend to cancel each other out. The method of scaling uses the best elements of each: the resulting set of scaled marks for each class has the average and spread of the marks of that class in the common examination, but the order of merit of the teachers' estimates. The scaled marks are the combination of two processes: *within classes* the teachers' estimates decide the relative position of individuals; *between classes* the common test decides the relative position of groups.

A very simple version of scaling is described in Yates and Pidgeon's *Admission to Grammar Schools* (1957). The teachers list the pupils' names in order of merit, according to their personal estimate of ability (column 1 below). A common test, preferably an objective attainment test, is given to pupils in all the schools concerned. (It is not necessary for pupils to write their names on this test: they need only write the name of the school, and of their class, if the scaling is done by classes.) The marks scored by each pupil in the common test are set out in column 2 below. These test scores are now rearranged in order of merit (column 3). To get the scaled marks, column 2 is removed and each child receives the mark now opposite his name. At first sight, this procedure seems monstrously unfair, but in fact it gives almost identical results to those calculated by complex statistical procedures.

| School A Class III | Teacher's order of merit | Test scores | Scaled marks |
|---|---|---|---|
| 1. | Charles | 69 | 71 |
| 2. | Edward | 71 | 69 |
| 3. | Yvonne | 65 | 67 |
| 4. | Christine | 60 | 65 |
| 5. | Jean | 67 | 64 |
| 6. | Peter | 64 | 60 |
|  | etc. | etc. | etc. |

Scaling by methods such as this (or by more sophisticated techniques) is an extremely useful device for making possible the use of the rich store of knowledge about pupils which would otherwise be locked away in school records or in the teachers' private judgements. Its use for CSE Mode 3 examinations offers an escape from the tyranny of external examinations. The CSE procedure is called *moderating*, since it is different from the simple scaling described above. A description of this procedure can be found in CSE Examination Bulletin No. 5 (1965) *School-based Examinations*.

Where the same examination has been given to all the pupils in an experiment or survey without the use of any standardized test, the problem of scaling disappears. But there still remains a serious obstacle to the use of marks derived from conventional examinations. Many studies have shown that such marks have poor reliability and there is rarely any evidence of validity.

SEMI–OBJECTIVE MARKING OF ESSAYS

There are three main sources of error in examination marks: variability in pupils' performance; subjectivity of marking; and the limitations of the conventional examination. The first of these can be dealt with either by giving a series of examinations, so that chance errors cancel out—an impossible burden on both pupils and teachers—or, preferably, by the use of teachers' estimates followed by an appropriate scaling procedure. The other two sources must be considered more fully.

We mentioned the problem of inaccurate marking earlier in the chapter. How are we to eliminate (or at least reduce) the errors which occur as a result of subjective marking, that is, marking in which the teacher makes a personal evaluation of an essay, or a drawing, or a cake or a piece of metal work? One of three ways can be followed or a combination of them, depending on the nature of the material to be assessed.

The standard method of controlling variation in marking is the use of a marking scheme. A research project which includes a subjective assessment of performance should borrow from the well-established practice of examiners by structuring the assessment according to a predetermined scheme. The assessment is divided into a number of categories or aspects; each of these is assessed in turn; and together they make up the general assessment. This has the advantage of permitting a more detailed analysis of the judgements in the research. If all the work is assessed on one aspect, and then on the second aspect, and so on, there is likely to be less 'halo' (allowing excellence in one respect to bias a judgement on a separate quality), and the effects of fatigue and mood will be distributed more widely, though they will not be eliminated. A marking scheme for children's composition devised by Schonell (1942, p. 484) provides an illustration. This form of distributed assessment for marking essays is familiar to most teachers, but this approach can also be applied to art and crafts or practical work (see p. 100).

The second method, also familiar to the experienced teacher, is multiple marking—the use of two or more markers working independently. Errors of judgement are diminished and sometimes cancel each other out, if the final mark is the sum of several assessments. There is also the advantage of providing a statistical check on the consistency of marking. The quick-impression procedure recommended by Wiseman (1949) is economical as well as efficient. Four markers make the assessments, working quickly on the basis of general impression. If a check shows that

*Schedule for marking written composition*

| | |
|---|---|
| A. Thought or content and vocabulary (12 marks) | 1. Clearness and continuity of thought<br>2. Originality of ideas<br>3. Interesting or uninteresting material<br>4. Use of words |
| B. Structure (7 marks) | 5. Variety of sentence: conjunctions and sentence patterns<br>6. Correctness of sentence structure<br>7. Paragraphing and general unity |
| C. Mechanical accuracy (6 marks) | 8. Spelling<br>9. Punctuation<br>10. Grammatical accuracy |

one marker is in clear disagreement with the other three, his assessments may be discarded altogether; but this may be unwise unless there is evidence that his judgements are less valid. It is at least possible that this marker is particularly perceptive, or unusually resistant to the false impression of neat handwriting or number of words in an essay, or smart finish and presentation of a piece of practical work. A thorough investigation of multiple marking of essays, including the factor of pupil variability, is described in CSE Examination Bulletin No. 12 (1966), *Multiple Marking of English Compositions*.

A third method is the use of a reference scale, composed of a series of 'model' examples to illustrate standards at each grade on the rating scale. This technique is sometimes used in the marking of compositions: for example, a discussion pamphlet prepared by the London Association for the Teaching of English (1965), *Assessing Compositions*, gives twenty-eight essays to illustrate standards of fifteen-year-old pupils as a guide in the assessment of imaginative writing at CSE standard. The essays are arranged in groups, from an E grade to an A. For practical work, a series of specimen pieces at each grade of performance helps to maintain a consistency of judgement. Each piece of work is matched with the piece of work on the scale which appears to be of equivalent standard, and the mark awarded is the mark at that point on the scale, just as is done in colour matching against a range of colours and hues. Though this is a crude device, its principal merit is that it prevents a 'drift' of standards when a large number of scripts have to be assessed in a short time.

The conventional essay-type examination is not generally a useful research instrument. Examinations may well be a necessary part of the general process of education, but the marks derived from essay examinations are ineffective in research studies because of their relatively low validity and reliability. There are various factors which are responsible. The design of most essay-type examinations restricts the sampling of a pupil's knowledge to that provided by the three or four essays which are required. The choice of questions which is usually offered increases difficulties in comparing candidates' attainments. There is also the difficulty of comparing essays which adopt very different approaches—the imaginative, fluent, slap-dash style and the meticulous, stiff and dull. The marks awarded to such contrasting essays may tell us more about the personality of the examiner than about the candidate's knowledge.

## SHORT-ANSWER QUESTIONS

If an area of the curriculum—particularly in secondary school work—has to be evaluated as part of a research project, the use of short-answer questions, at least as part of the examination, will increase the area of knowledge sampled by the test and can even give a better indication of reasoning power if the questions are properly constructed. Short-answer questions need not be in multiple-choice form; they can be open-ended, without complicating the marking unduly.

Common objections to the use of short-answer questions are that they measure only factual knowledge, and so encourage the wrong kind of study; that they fail to test the capacity to select and organize the material of an answer; and that they favour the pupil with slickness or speed or the grasshopper mentality. None of these defects *need* apply, if questions are carefully designed to avoid the dangers. Devising good questions takes time, but this may well be balanced by time saved in the actual marking. For example, an essay-type question, 'Outline the procedure for testing (some process in chemistry)', which requires twenty minutes, may be replaced by five short questions of the type: 'Describe the first stage (or the first two stages) in the procedure ...', etc. Another question, 'Discuss the factors (or events or considerations) which led up to (some historical event or decision)' may be replaced by: 'Which of the following were influential in ....', etc., followed by a list from which the candidate must make an appropriate selection. Examples of types of question which demand reasoning, application of principles or analysis of problems are given in CSE Examination Bulletin No. 4 (1964), *An Introduction to Objective-type Examinations.*

A test of this kind need not depend on speed, if a generous time-limit is set. If marks tend to be high in consequence, they can be scaled into grades, and the resulting grades will give a more reliable assessment than an essay examination covering the same period of time. Some scaling will be necessary in any case if scores on a short-answer examination are combined with essay marks because of the probable use of quite different ranges in marking. For certain types of material, essay questions are still necessary. A mixture of the two types may produce the most appropriate test: short answers for testing knowledge, application and analysis; essays for synthesis, evaluation and judgement. One advantage of a short-answer component in an examination taken by a large number of candidates is that the scores in the short-answer section can be used as an objective basis for scaling (or for checking) the more subjective marking of the essay-type questions.

The construction of a short-answer examination should be done systematically, since so much depends on the quality of the questions. This procedure is also outlined in CSE Examination Bulletin No. 4 (1964). In stage 1 the areas to be covered by the examination, or the objectives of the course, are noted, and their relative importance is decided. Stage 2 is the provisional formulation of questions, making sure that more are invented than will in fact be required. Experience in this field suggests that this is best done as a team effort by a group who try out possible versions on each other. In stage 3, a selection of questions is made, so that the number of questions on each aspect is roughly proportional to the importance of that aspect, as determined in the first stage. Stage 4 consists of arranging the selected items in an appropriate sequence, formulating the instructions, deciding the instructions, deciding the lay-out, and checking that none of the questions gives clues to the correct answer to another. Although this last stage is just a matter of checking details, it is none the less important.

If the test is to be used on a scale large enough to justify the expense, the remaining stages should apply the procedure of item analysis outlined in the appendix to the previous chapter. The draft version of the test is given a pilot run, and the level of difficulty and discriminative power of each item is checked by item analysis. Where multiple-choice questions have been used, the analysis of data from the pilot run will ensure that the alternatives offered are all feasible: any alternative which is rejected by all candidates is useless. If a pilot run is impracticable, the item analysis should be carried out after the test has been given. Items which are shown to be invalid can be omitted from the total score, and, if the test is repeated, a shortened version may be used.

With a single class the teacher can rapidly complete the whole procedure of item analysis by a short-cut classroom method described in *Short-Cut Statistics for Teacher-Made Tests* (Educational Testing Service, 1964). After marking the tests, the teacher divides the papers into two equal piles, the upper half on total score and the lower half. If there is an odd number of pupils in the class, the script with the median mark is omitted. The teacher continues by distributing one pile to the pupils on his right, the other pile to those on his left: a pupil is designated teller for each half. When the teacher calls out 'one', pupils who have a paper on which item 1 is correct raise their hands. The tellers count and announce the number in each half, and the teacher records the two numbers in columns headed H (higher) and L (lower). The procedure is repeated for the remaining items. Finally, the sum of H plus L, multiplied by 100 and divided by the number of pupils in the class, gives the percentage difficulty level of each item, taken separately; the difference (H minus L), multiplied by 100 and divided by half the number in the class, gives an index of discrimination, equivalent to that described in the appendix to chapter 8.

UNSCALED EXAMINATION MARKS

It is sometimes impossible for the research worker either to scale the marks available or to administer a satisfactory common test. Where a retrospective assessment is required, as for example if a measure of secondary school attainment is to be used in a study of university students, it is necessary to fall back on such records of examination marks as are available. If these records are of class examinations, the marks are useless, since there is no common standard. National examinations, for the General Certificate of Education or the Scottish Certificate of Education, are marked on a common standard, with the intention that an 'A' grade from one Board or in one subject indicates the same degree of excellence as from another. This is an assumption only, but since university admission procedures treat the marks as equivalent, it is often a necessary assumption. There remains the problem of combining a group of marks in, say, three A-level examinations, or in five Scottish Higher grade passes, into a single assessment of secondary school performance. In a combination of three A-level passes, do two A grades and one D represent a better or worse performance than one A and two B grades? The Universities Central Council on Admissions (UCCA) has adopted a classification which should introduce a standard procedure to deal with this problem. Thus, for a combination of three A-level passes, class 1:3 includes the following sets of grades: AAA, AAB, AAC, ABB; class 2:3 includes AAD, ABC, BBB, AAE, ABD, ACC, BBC, ABE, ACD, BBD, BCC; and so on. The answer to the question above is that, on this scale, ABB, is superior to AAD. The details of the UCCA classification can be derived from the tables in their statistical returns, which are published annually.

With Scottish Certificate passes, previous research studies have used a simple procedure of counting a Higher grade pass as 2 and an Ordinary grade as 1, excluding Ordinary grade passes in which the student also has an H pass. This is too crude, and is probably little better than a straight count of the number of Higher passes. A system is needed which will take account of the marks in each subject and give a ranking of students with three, four, five or six Highers at different levels of mark; but it is difficult to devise, and it will be difficult to establish the validity of any such system.

Little research has been done on the question of the best way to use these Certificate passes and marks. School records remain a relatively unexploited source of information, but what has been said in this chapter shows that there are serious obstacles to their effective use in educational research.

SUMMARY

It is often difficult to use examination marks in research studies. Markers use different standards, which prevent comparisons between classes from being meaningful. Such marks can be made equivalent by one of the simple methods of scaling in which a common test is given to all the pupils and the examination marks for each class are related to this standard. If a suitable published test is not available, the research worker may have to design his own examination. If essays are used, a marking scheme or multiple marking improves the reliability of the marks. Short-answer tests can be marked more objectively, but pilot runs of such tests are important and should lead, where possible, to item analysis and checks on validity.

The use of examination marks without scaling procedures is only justified where a common standard can be assumed. GCE and SCE grades are often used in research on secondary school attainment or in the validation of university selection methods.

| Creativity and
Divergent Thinking

Assessment of the results of an experiment or a new curriculum should not be restricted to tests and examinations. These measure what Guilford (1950) called convergent behaviour, the ability to give the correct answer. There are occasions when we also wish to measure divergent behaviour, the ability to give an original or unusual answer. Learning, in the simple sense of getting to know the correct answer to a problem or the facts of a situation, is still the major objective of education. But to aim at this directly, without consideration of attitudes engendered by the process of instruction or of the need to stimulate independent thinking, may defeat its own purpose, if it discourages pupils from being active agents in their own education. This suggests that the assessment of children's performance should often include more than the tests of ability and attainment which have been described in chapters 8 and 9. The measurement of attitudes and personality is discussed in chapters 11 and 12. This chapter reviews the testing of creative responses, and includes also projective techniques, which, though they belong properly to the area of personality assessment, remain essentially similar to many tests of creativity and provide useful research measurements on a wide range of topics.

Goldman (1964) described 'creativity' as 'an umbrella term . . . used rather loosely to describe original, inventive and novel productions of thought'. The use of the word is sometimes 'so wide as to mean nothing'. Essentially, a test of creative thinking is not so much concerned with whether answers are right or wrong as with whether the responses are fluent or restricted, and original or conventional. The term covers a range of abilities which have not been precisely identified by research. This aspect of mental ability has not been altogether ignored in the past by psychologists. Binet's original intelligence test in 1905 included a test of fluency ('Give me as many words as you possibly can in three minutes'); but he was concerned only with the total number of words. Since 1950, there has been a steady growth of interest in the concept of creativity. The Minnesota Tests of Creative Thinking (Torrance, 1962) and Hudson's *Contrary Imaginations* (1966) and *Frames of Mind* (1968) in Britain provide examples of measurement techniques. A common form of question is: 'Think of as many different (or unusual) uses as you can for a brick'. An alternative approach is to ask for as many meanings of words as possible. Whatever open-ended stimulus is used, it may be applied with or without a time-limit and under examination conditions or informally. The conditions will, of course, affect the results.

Hudson (1966, pp. 90–1)* shows the enormous differences in response between intelligent schoolboys when asked for possible uses of certain everyday objects:

'At the one extreme, (there was) a mathematical near-prodigy, with an I.Q. well within the top 10 per cent of the Cambridge population, and open-ended responses as follows:

(Barrel) Keeping wine in, playing football
(Paper clip) Keeping papers together, repairing page of a book
(Tin of boot polish) Cleaning shoes, (when empty) keeping pins, etc.
(Brick) Building things, throwing
(Blanket) Keeping warm, smothering fire, tying to trees and sleeping in (as a hammock), improvised stretcher

And at the other end of the scale, the slightly awe-inspiring spectacle of a fluent mind in spate:

(Barrel) For storing old clothes, shoes, tools, paper, etc. For pickling onions in. For growing a yew-tree in. For inverting and sitting on. As a table. As firewood chopped up. As a drain or

* Reprinted from HUDSON, L., *Contrary Imaginations*, 1966, by permission of the author, Methuen & Co. Ltd and Schocken Books Inc., New York.

sump for rain water. As a sand pit. At a party for games. For making cider or beer in. As a play-pen for a small child. As a rabbit hutch, inverted with a door out of the side. On top of a pole as a dove cot. Let into a wall as a night exit for a dog or a cat. As the base for a large lamp. As a vase for golden rod and michaelmas daisies, as an ornament, especially if it is a small one. With holes cut in the top and sides, either for growing wallflowers and strawberries in, or for stacking pots, and kitchen utensils. As a proper garbage can or wastepaper basket. As a ladder to reach the top shelves of a high bookcase. As a casing for a home-made bomb. Sawn in half, as a doll's crib. As a drum. As a large birds' nest.

(Paper clip) For holding papers together. To clean wax out of one's ears. Red hot, to bore holes in a cork. Unwound, as a pin or needle for rough work. To clean the dirt from between floorboards, and from under finger-nails. As a fuse wire. As a keeper for a magnet. As a safety-pin. As a hair clip. As a tooth pick. As a stylus for working on wax or in clay. As a fish-hook. With a thread passed through it as a sort of hook. As a charm on a necklace or bracklet. As a collar for a pet mouse, or as a ring for a bird's ankle. To tie labels on with. Unwound, to clear out a small hole, bind something together or as a solder wire. As a sort of shoe-lace. As a tiepin. As a means of barter. As a counter in a game of cards. As a piece of a board game such as draughts. As confetti. To sabotage a clock. To match with a spring. To make into chain mail.'

This 'diverger' was equally fluent in imagining uses (and abuses) of the remaining objects.

Scoring the responses is also a problem. Do you count all responses, possible and impossible, or must the uses be realistic? Do you score just for the *number* of uses suggested or also for the *quality* of the suggestions? Can there be a scale of originality in terms of uses of objects? Different research workers have approached these problems in different ways: at present there can be no agreed principles to pass on to others. All the scoring schemes are to some extent unsatisfactory; they are also laborious.

A more serious problem is the question of what is in fact measured by such tests: do they measure one quality of mind (or, technically, one factor) or many different and loosely related qualities; to what extent do they overlap with tests of intelligence or verbal ability; and, most important of all, is the ability to produce fluent and original responses an indication of that creative genius which is so valuable a quality in design, invention and problem solving at the highest level of intelligence in adult life? It is possible that these tests of divergent thinking are related only to a person's fantasy world and give little indication of that individual's capacity for *realistic* invention. For a further discussion of how to interpret tests of creativity and a description of other similar tests, the reader is referred to C. W. Taylor's (1964) *Creativity; Progress and Potential*, or to Wallach and Kogan's (1965) *Modes of Thinking in Young Children*. Butcher (1968) provides a straightforward summary of the research into possible connections between creativity and intelligence.

At present, applied to schoolchildren, the tests are of interest in that they explore an area of performance and ability which tends to be neglected by the conventional tests of convergent thinking. Consequently, they may be relevant to certain aspects of the evaluation of new curricula or to the assessment of 'progressive' schemes of work, which include among their objectives the encouragement of original and imaginative thinking. As research on creativity develops, new problems open up. For example, Torrance (1963) reports four ages when the growth of creativity suffers a check, 5, 9, 13, 17. He interprets this as attributable to certain social and cultural pressures including emphasis on differing sex roles, and links this finding with the question of why are there so few women inventors.

It seems reasonable to assume that whether or not creativity is a separate intellectual dimension, there is almost certainly a link between creativity and personality. Even the methods of measurement overlap. One of the tests of divergent thinking used by Hudson (1966) asks the pupil to illustrate the title 'ZEBRA CROSSING'. A common approach to personality measurement uses a picture of an everyday situation and asks the subject to describe what happened next. The responses would be interpreted as evidence of that person's personality. This would be called a *projective* test—scored and interpreted in a different way, the responses might also indicate divergent thinking.

## PROJECTIVE TECHNIQUES

The measurement of creativity is a comparatively recent development: projective techniques have a much longer history in psychology and represent a different type of inquiry. The basic principle is that an ambiguous stimulus is presented—a picture or an ink-blot or an incomplete sentence—and the response which a subject gives provides a clue to the way in which the stimulus is perceived, and thus to his personality or attitude. The experimenter is not concerned with right or wrong answers, but with whether the response is normal or abnormal—that is, frequent and conventional, or rare and unusual. The Word Association game is an early form: 'Say the first word which occurs to you when I say "black".' (The normal response is 'white'.) Among the best-known projective measures is the Rorschach Inkblots, which dates from 1911. Murray's Thematic Apperception Test (TAT) (1943) is one example of many which use the 'picture story' technique: the subject makes up a story from pictures which he is shown, and the themes he chooses, and the particular 'needs' or 'presses' which the characters express are an indication of his own personality structure. L. Jackson's *Test of Family Attitudes* (1952) uses drawings in this way to draw out the feelings which a child has to members of his family. Lowenfeld used Mosaic designs, or a sand-tray with toys.

'Projection' is a psychoanalytic term, used to indicate the process by which inner tensions find expression in our relations with external objects. Interpretation of projective material necessitates the acceptance of some psychological theory or explanation of this process. Consequently, it is not a task for the amateur psychologist: training in the application and interpretation of projective tests is necessary. Interpretation is often subjective, based on evidence which to the layman may appear ambiguous. Consequently, if projective techniques are used in a research project, the material should be interpreted independently by at least two persons so that a check can be made on inter-marker reliability.

However, the technique can be used to advantage in educational research, and provided due caution is observed in interpreting the results and no attempt is made to invoke complex psychological explanation, it is a quick and inexpensive method of collecting information. (The ease in obtaining the information must be balanced against the difficulty of interpreting it.)

Sentence completion, for example, is a convenient device in questionnaires, or for the exploration of attitudes or opinions where it is important to avoid giving an indication of the kind of reply expected. In evaluating a course of instruction, a teacher may ask his students or pupils to complete the sentence: 'The best thing about this course was. . . .' or 'The course was. . . .' He may be surprised at some of the responses; if so, he must recognize that these responses represent the first ideas which arise when the student thinks about the course—though they may also represent an attempt to be smart or cynical. In a more general context, sentences may take an even more open form: 'School is. . . .' or 'Teachers. . . .' or 'When I went into the mathematics class. . . .'

Classifying responses is a key part of any research procedure. Responses to the sentences above may be classified as emotive or neutral, and if they are emotive, they can be sub-classified as favourable or hostile. Even this limited imposition of structure in analysis of responses may prove to be too subjective, as will be shown when a second assessor independently reviews the material. A straight count of the frequency of various responses, or content analysis, also raises questions of how to group and classify. The technique is an open, exploratory one, and absence of structure is an inherent element, so that the technique is often more appropriate to the early stages of a research; in the later stages a more precise method may be built up out of the rich material which the open approach produces.

A particularly promising adaptation of the projective method is the use of children's compositions. There are many versions possible here, depending on the age and literacy of the children and the objectives of the research. Young children may be asked to draw a picture and tell a story about it. With even younger children, playing with toys, accompanied by a running narrative, is essentially the same technique, but this is really a clinical procedure for which training and experience are needed. With older children, the conventional composition or essay provides material which has not received the attention it deserves from research workers as a means of gathering relevant data. An element of structuring in the instructions for the composition helps the children to write and the investigator to classify the results. Not every composition topic is suitable, of course; some topics may be regarded by a school as too private or personal. All research material from children should be treated as strictly confidential; but parents have a right to protest if children are asked to give information on topics which go beyond the reasonable limits of inquiry. A good example of the proper use of this method is to be found in Veness (1962). A modified version of Veness' method was used by the authors in their inquiry into transfer to secondary school. Primary school children were asked: 'Imagine that you are quite old, at least 40 years old. Look back over your life and write a story about what has happened to you and what you have done during these years'. Following this there was a series of prompting questions such as: 'When did you leave school?' and 'What job did you do?' These were added to ensure that the material could be used for a measure of level of ambition. Examples of how this was done are given in Nisbet and Entwistle's *The Transition to Secondary Education* (1969, ch. 4).

A similar technique was used some six weeks after the pupils had begun their secondary school careers. They were asked to describe their experiences in the first few weeks at secondary school, again in a structured essay form. An analysis of these essays provided one method of judging how many of the pupils had experienced difficulties or anxieties in adjusting to the transition. Excerpts from the essays are given in chapter 9 of the report cited above.

There is one obvious defect in this method. One can never be sure whether the results show merely how the children have been taught to write, whether they will express what they truly feel or expect, whether they are merely copying some story or television incident which has caught their fancy. In the inquiry mentioned above, the essays of children who entered one school under a new procedure were compared with essays from a previous year-group when a different procedure operated. A comparison of this kind (which revealed significant differences) carries more conviction than a simple analysis of one set of essays. Against this clear weakness of the technique must be set one major advantage, namely, that the essay method is often acceptable to schools as a part of school work—more acceptable, certainly, than inventories and attitude scales. With imagination, the research worker should be able to devise new ways of exploiting this technique. In the end, it remains a subjective method; and for many studies the more precise methods described in chapter 11 and 12 will be preferable.

## SUMMARY

Most intellectual tests ask the pupil to think convergently towards a single correct or best answer. Tests of creativity measure the ability to think divergently, drawing on unusual or original responses. Such tests of divergent thinking are a recent development and methods of scoring are not well developed. Some of the earliest attempts at measuring personality used the 'projective' technique, which is essentially similar. Subjects are presented with an ambiguous stimulus—such as an ink-blot—and personality dimensions are inferred from a categorization of the responses. Open-ended questions and the use of children's essays to measure attitudes illustrate other ways of using pupils' unrestricted answers.

| Personality Assessment

When discussing children's behaviour in the classroom, teachers soon find it necessary to use the term 'personality' to explain why children react in their own characteristic ways to common situations. It is not always clear what is meant by personality. Allport's definition (1961) is often quoted:

> Personality is the dynamic organization within the individual of those psychophysical systems that determine his characteristic behaviour and thought.

This definition emphasizes the distinct differences in personality that exist between people, and the adjective 'dynamic' underlines the fact that personality is not a fixed entity but will change as a result of experience. Allport also acknowledged that it is possible to identify certain basic similarities or consistent patterns in personality. He concluded that in personality a man is to some extent like all other men; he is also like certain limited groups of men; but finally he is an individual unlike all other men. In a group, one tends to notice the ways in which people differ. Educational research, however, has to use systems of classifying or grouping together children who show common patterns of behaviour, who tend to behave in similar ways or show common 'source traits' (Cattell, 1965).

Cattell and Guilford in the United States and Eysenck in Britain have been foremost in their attempts to measure common personality traits. Among the dimensions of personality most frequently used in educational research in this country are 'emotional instability' (neuroticism or anxiety) and 'extraversion'. Other investigators, using Cattell's (1956, 1963) scales, the *16-PF Scale* and the *Children's Personality Questionnaire*, measure up to sixteen dimensions (including intelligence) identified by Cattell.

His list is based on traits characterized by opposite types of behaviour: for example, reserved–outgoing, emotional–stable, humble–assertive, tough-minded–tender-minded, trusting–suspicious.

Personality dimensions can be assessed in a variety of ways. There are different names for the form in which the information is collected—inventory, scale, questionnaire: but a more convenient classification is to distinguish (*a*) self-rating procedures and (*b*) ratings by others (see p. 119–20).

SELF-RATING PROCEDURES

Certain aspects of personality can be measured from the answers given by people to questions about themselves or about their probable behaviour in specific situations. Such questions may be either explicit or implicit. The term *explicit* applies to a scale in which a person rates himself on a series of dimensions which he can be expected to understand and where there is no attempt to conceal what is being assessed. In its simplest form, this is the popular 'women's magazine' approach.

'Are you a good mixer?
1. If you are in a group discussing a topic with which you are unfamiliar, do you (*a*) keep silent, (*b*) join in, (*c*) change the subject?
2. If you disagree with what someone says, do you (*a*) say you disagree, (*b*) pretend to agree, (*c*) express no opinion?'

This is seldom adequate except for the most superficial description of personality. Individual items have low reliability; a scale made up of a series of items is necessary. But to justify adding together the answers to questions like these, a preliminary trial would be necessary, to check that certain answers go together—for example, that those who answer 1(*a*) also tend to answer 2(*c*). In effect this would lead to a full item analysis, but such lengthy methods are hardly justified where explicit questions have been used. In some ways, however, this simplicity of approach might seem to be a point of strength. It apparently provides magazine readers with a stimulus towards greater self-knowledge, and, since the conclusions are self evident, the person might well be led to obtain advice. There is a serious snag. The use of explicit questions depends heavily on self-knowledge and insight for achieving accurate descriptions of personality. Thus the person who gives perceptive replies must already have adequate self-knowledge and insight. The justification of use of explicit questioning as a procedure to aid self-knowledge relies, in fact, on a circular argument. Also, the dimensions of personality which have been recognized by everyday contact and embodied in the words of the English language are too vague and overlap too much to be really effective in research. (Also, different concepts and different words have evolved in other languages.)

The *implicit* approach to personality measurement also relies on self-knowledge, but is less affected by the desire to show oneself in a favourable light. Cattell's and Eysenck's inventories again contain questions about people's behaviour, but these are designed to make it difficult to see which type of behaviour is socially desirable. It is also impossible for most people to guess the psychological dimensions which lie behind the questions. The dimensions of personality are derived from an analysis of responses, and are not obvious from the questions. A caricature of this approach is expressed in the popular stereotype of the psychologist, who is supposed to be able to draw profound psychological conclusions from the answer to a simple question like 'Do you prefer soft-centred chocolates?' But answers to questions such as 'Do you like surprises?', 'Do you enjoy an argument?', 'Do you often feel bored?', though having relatively little significance by themselves, may be put together to chart an outline of personality structure. Surveying an area of unmapped country involves a succession of measurements from different positions, and a complex process of calculation to fit these measurements together.

The projective tests described in chapter 10 certainly used an implicit approach. Applying an ambiguous stimulus, such as an ink-blot, has no obvious relation to personality. The difference between the clinical and the statistical approach to personality assessment is still wide. The clinician makes use of the ambiguous stimulus in the light of his own experience. The statistical psychologist applies the implicit questions to a large sample of normal people and tries to discover patterns in the way the responses are made.

The search for questions which will effectively discriminate between personality types without being patently obvious to the non-psychologist, or to the subject who wishes to convey a socially acceptable impression, has made relatively slow progress. Interpretation of answers depends to some extent on the basic theory of personality which one accepts. An objective statistical analysis of the pattern of responses to a series of questions like this is, to some extent, independent of the theory of personality accepted. It is not entirely independent, since the initial choice of questions must be made from some theoretical standpoint.

The obvious complexity of personality assessment by indirect or 'implicit' questioning should deter anyone who is planning research on a relatively small scale from trying to develop his own test of personality in this way. It is advisable to use either one of the rating methods, discussed towards the end of the chapter, or one of the standard personality scales which use implicit questioning. Details of these scales can be found in the *Mental Measurements Yearbook* or in the more general texts mentioned in chapter 8. But before selecting a test of personality for use in a research project, it is important to consider the evidence of reliability and validity given in the manual. Reliability coefficients in personality tests tend to be much lower than those found with intellectual tests. The researcher will have to be satisfied with test re-test correlations of about 0·75 or 0·80, though this implies that the measures will only be useful with large groups of children—the tests will provide little useful information about the individual.

The evidence of validity is most important. This may be presented in the form of direct evidence of external validity, when the test has been shown to discriminate effectively between groups of persons who are known to be quite different in at least one dimension of personality. For example, Eysenck has given his test, the *Eysenck Personality Inventory*, to groups of neurotics as well as to normal people. The fact that the neurotics were found to have much higher scores on 'neuroticism' as measured by the test is reassuring. It is not easy to make such direct checks on validity for most personality dimensions, where behavioural differences do not lead to medical diagnosis. The evidence of validity has then to be indirect, by showing either that the scale as a whole assesses certain dimensions common to other established personality measures or that the individual items work together to locate a definite personality trait.

This internal consistency is usually checked by a method of item analysis similar to that already described in the appendix to chapter 8. Careful validation is one of the hall-marks of any good test.

Even when a well-validated test has been used, there may still be problems of interpretation. The field of personality is one where, without a knowledge of psychology based on more than just a superficial study, the research worker will find many pitfalls, both in the application and in the interpretation of personality measures. A special danger is what might be termed the *jingle fallacy*, the error of assuming that a test measures what its title says it measures. Even though the items in a scale or inventory may appear to be relevant to the quality being assessed —having, in technical terms, *face validity*—they may be measuring the intelligence of the subject in guessing the responses approved or expected, or the extent to which he is willing to commit himself, or even his attitude to psychology and psychologists.

Another danger in the interpretation of inventory responses concerns the validity of assuming that what people say is a measure of what they do. It is easy to fake responses in a self-rating scale, and even when a person tries to be sincere, he is liable to distort his replies to present a socially acceptable impression. Self-rating procedures are therefore seldom of use in a competitive situation, such as in selection. In non-competitive situations, highly educated persons report themselves as more neurotic than those with minimal education, but this may be only because they are more willing to give frank answers. Many people do not know themselves well enough to give valid responses to items on personality, or are not sufficiently sensitive or thoughtful and consequently give superficial replies which merely reflect fashions or stereotypes.

With young children, the validity of self-rating is open to question, and a teacher's rating of personality is commonly used. This leads to the alternative approach to personality testing mentioned earlier in the chapter.

RATINGS BY OTHERS

One method of obtaining personality assessments—an old-fashioned method, but none the worse for that—is to ask a responsible, intelligent and perceptive person to make a judgement of the subject's personality in a form which permits comparison with others. A straightforward example is the teacher's 'mark' of A, B, C, etc., for good conduct or application to school work. If only one class is involved, it is possible for one teacher to make assessments which permit comparisons within that class. With larger numbers, problems arise: how can we ensure that one teacher's ratings are based on the same standard as another teacher's, or even that they are judging the same things? 'Good conduct' to one may mean a quiet docility, to the other constructive participation in group work. These are the problems of comparability and subjectivity of ratings.

A rating of one person by another is influenced by the personality of the rater as well as that of the person being rated. It is the product of an interaction. (Little consideration in educational research has been given to the implications of this: a pupil or student may in fact respond differently to different tutors.) An effective rating scale must therefore seek to remove personal differences between raters. A second problem is the problem of 'halo', that is, the tendency for a good (or bad) rating on one aspect, such as intelligence, to influence unduly the ratings on other aspects, such as application to work, interest in work, parental encouragement, stability, originality and so on. Teacher's ratings of such qualities show a closer correlation than objective measures, possibly because their ratings are more valid and the qualities are closely interrelated, but possibly also because of 'halo'. One form of halo effect, probably not as serious as is sometimes alleged, is the tendency for teachers to give unduly favourable ratings to pupils who have the 'middle-class' qualities of good manners, good speech and smart appearance. A further problem arises when one person is required to make a large number of ratings, or to make ratings over a long period of time. He must somehow be consistent and maintain equivalent standards. The problems are similar to those discussed in chapter 9, when the question of comparability of examination marks was reviewed. The procedures commonly adopted for ratings, however, are different from those applied to marks in examinations.

## SYSTEMATIC RATING SCHEMES

The first step is to define carefully the quality to be assessed. Vague terms like 'maturity' which are open to varying interpretations must be avoided, and technical terms like 'introversion' should not be used, for the same reason. A description should be in simple words, however difficult this may be, and it should be in what is called 'behavioural terms', that is, by reference to actual observable actions rather than by abstract nouns. Such written descriptions do help to reduce the halo effect. But halo is best controlled if the raters are given precise instructions on how to make their ratings. If a teacher is asked to rate his pupils on a number of qualities, he should be asked to rate all the pupils on one aspect first, before rating them on the next aspect. Obviously this will not remove the halo effect, but it may help to reduce it. The lay-out of the paper on which the ratings are made will affect the way in which they are made. The simplest arrangement—a column of names and columns for ratings, or a page for each pupil containing all the rating scales—invites the teacher to assess the pupils one at a time on *all* aspects. Separate pages for each rating are preferable; or, if the number is small, the pupils' names are written on cards which are sorted in categories for one rating, the ratings noted, and then the cards are shuffled in preparation for the next rating. (Elaborate procedures, however, may go beyond the extent to which an experimenter can hope to maintain a teacher's good will.)

Not only should the general quality be defined, but each interval or category in whatever rating scale is used must be described so as to indicate precisely what degree of excellence or deficit is implied at each point. Many sound rating scales have been devised and are described in books on guidance and selection. The research worker is well advised at least to consult this material before embarking on a scale of his own. For example, a specimen follow-up report form for Civil Service personnel, quoted by Anstey (1966, p. 203) includes the following items:

| X | X applies | Tendency to X | Average | Tendency to Y | Y applies | Y |
|---|---|---|---|---|---|---|
| 2. Extremely quick in the uptake | ... | ... | ... | ... | ... | Does not always grasp the point |
| 4. Tackles any job in a most direct and orderly manner | ... | ... | ... | ... | ... | Approach to work rather haphazard |

A simple rating scale, used in the research project referred to in chapter 10 (Nisbet and Entwistle, 1969), assessed pupils' attitude to work as rated by their teachers:

| Rating | Attitude to work |
|---|---|
| 1 | Absolutely absorbed in work, likes to excel, excellent power of sustained attention, does extra work in school and at home. |

| Rating | Attitude to work |
|---|---|
| 2 | Very interested and absorbed in most of the work set, likes to do well. |
| 3 | Normally interested and attentive. |
| 4 | Interested in little of the work done, shows weak power of attention. |
| 5 | Indifferent to any work, never really absorbed by school activities. |

The wording here may be criticized as still rather general, except for rating 1. The use of a five-point scale is considered by some to encourage a skewed distribution. The lowest grade is used too seldom, and all doubtful ratings are given 3 as a safe average. The value of a scale depends on its spreading out the sample being assessed, and too many or too few in any one category diminishes the efficiency of the scale. A four-point scale forces the rater to decide whether a person is above or below average on the trait; and an appropriate choice of wording can correct the usual bias towards generosity which results in an uneven distribution among the categories.

An alternative method of ensuring use of the full range of the rating scale is to specify the percentage distribution of grades to be assigned:

| A | B | C | D | E |
|---|---|---|---|---|
| 10% | 20% | 40% | 20% | 10% |

Usually teachers resent a fixed percentage, arguing (often correctly) that each class is quite different in its range and distribution of whatever quality is to be rated. The bias towards generosity which has been mentioned appears in the finding that, in use of the above scale, the E grades usually amount to less than 10 per cent. If a number of classes are being rated, especially in a school where streaming applies, an insistence on a fixed distribution in each class is absurd. It is in fact permissible if the statistical analysis is separate for each class, but teachers are not easily persuaded of such points.

In some studies a simpler procedure, ranking, is all that is required. Here the teacher is required to arrange his class in an order, from one extreme to the other. This can be a difficult task unless guidance is given. For example, the teacher of physical education is asked to rank an adolescent class in order of physical maturity. Two lines are drawn across the page on which the names of pupils are to be written in rank order. The teacher is asked first to write above the top line the names of those whose physical development is most advanced; and then to write below the second line the names of those who are least developed. (Precise guidance must be given on which aspects of physical development are to be considered.) In the space between the two lines, he then writes beside but below the upper line the names of those whom he considers might be included in the highest category; and similarly beside but above the lower line those who might be considered for the lowest category. Lines are drawn to mark off these last two groups, and the remaining names are written in the middle. This gives a five-point grading, but, if the teacher is willing to continue, he is asked to number the pupils in rank order within each category. As was said previously in another context, a balance has to be struck between precision and practicality; for without the willing participation of those for whom a research project is an added task with no return, no precision of assessment can be expected.

The application of these rating or ranking procedures should incorporate a check on validity and reliability—by asking two teachers to rate the same class and comparing their assessments, by repeating the ratings from one teacher (or several) after an interval as a check on consistency, or by comparing the ratings with some objective criterion, even if this can be done only for a small proportion of the pupils.

Ratings can be used to advantage in a wide variety of situations. Selection interviews, for example, may be made less subjective, if each member of the interviewing board fills in a rating form covering a range of relevant qualities for each candidate. The form obliges the board to take account of aspects to be noted, directs attention to relevant behaviour, reduces halo effect, and provides evidence for a follow-up to check on the relevance of the qualities listed and the judgement of the board members.

This summary of personality measures covers only some of the methods available. Assessment of attitudes (chapter 12) overlaps the content of this chapter and developmental scales (chapter 13) might also be linked with personality measures.

SUMMARY

Self-report inventories and ratings by others form distinct approaches to personality assessment. Self-report inventories may be made up from questions which are explicit or implicit. With explicit items, the purpose of the question is obvious and this may bias the findings. Inventories using implicit items, after statistical analyses and careful validation, provide measures of various personality dimensions such as 'neuroticism' and 'extra-version'. The results from such inventories should be interpreted carefully, avoiding the 'jingle' fallacy. Ratings by others, in particular by teachers or parents, can be useful in educational research, but only if systematic rating scales are produced. In this way the ratings from different people can be treated as being comparable.

## CHAPTER 12

Attitude Measurement

The technique of measuring attitudes and personality have much in common, but, as attitudes tend to be specific rather than general, the research worker is often faced with the problem of developing his own scale. This is a more practicable task than developing a general personality test or inventory, because it is easier to define what is being measured in a specific attitude scale. We can accept that people vary in their attitude to this or that matter without committing ourselves to a complex theory of personality. But this very specificity indicates that attitude scales have a limited range of usefulness. Vernon (1953) stressed the attachment of attitudes to specific contexts when he attempted to define what is an attitude. 'There is no agreed definition,' he wrote. 'But in this context it generally implies a personality disposition or drive which determines behaviour towards, or opinions and beliefs about, a certain type of person, object, situation, institution or concept' (p. 144). The measurement of attitudes demands a knowledge of appropriate techniques of construction; these are described in this chapter. But the use of specific attitude scales also carries with it a risk of superficiality; it is important to ensure that the attitude dimensions measured are related to a sound theoretical framework, through an understanding of the problem being investigated.

Well-constructed attitude scales are available in a number of areas: Eysenck's scales of tough- and tender-mindedness, and of radicalism and conservatism, are examples in the area of social attitudes; and the Minnesota Teacher Attitude Inventory gives a measure of progressive and traditional attitudes to teaching. The General Anxiety Scale and Test Anxiety Scale for Children (GASC and TASC) designed by Sarason (1960) can be used to assess children's attitudes to school pressures. Such scales or inventories occupy a position midway between personality assessment and attitude measurement; the GASC in particular could readily have been included in the previous chapter. But if we wish to measure the attitudes of fifth-formers to science, or to a new science syllabus which has been introduced, then a scale must be constructed specifically for this purpose.

There is a choice of techniques available for constructing an attitude scale. Several of these are well developed and well established, some having a relatively long history, such as Thurstone's method which dates from 1928. A detailed account of the statistical procedures involved in these various methods is to be found in Edwards' (1957) *Techniques of Attitude Scale Construction*. Vernon (1953), in *Personality Tests and Assessments* (chapter 9), gives a lucid summary of techniques, with examples of scales in use, specimen items, and non-mathematical explanation of the construction procedures.

The basic pattern of most attitude scales is a series of statements, all relating to one clearly defined topic and expressing favourable, neutral or unfavourable attitudes to it. The person to whom the scale is applied indicates whether or not he agrees with the statements, or how strongly he agrees or disagrees, or which statement expresses his attitude best. The resulting score shows the person's attitude as a position on a scale ranging from strongly favourable through neutral to strongly opposed. The statements must be carefully selected if they are to constitute an effective scale, and statistical procedures are used to check that certain principles of selection are being properly applied. No single technique is the best in all situations, and it is often advisable to use alternative approaches to the measurement of attitude as a check on the validity of the measures. But a score on one scale cannot readily be compared directly with a score on another. Their measurements are relative, and the proper use of an attitude scale is to allow comparisons of the attitudes of different groups or of individuals compared with that of groups, or to assess the effect on attitudes of changes in, say, a school curriculum.

THURSTONE SCALE

The construction of a Thurstone-type scale starts with the collection of a large number of statements expressing some attitude to the topic under consideration. If, for example, we wish to assess the attitudes of undergraduate students to teaching as a career, preliminary discussion with students will produce a variety of statements, and scanning the literature will add to the collection. If the scale is to be applied to children, the use of children's essays as a source for statements helps to ensure that the wording is appropriate for children. Other statements will have to be invented, until upwards of 100 such statements are available, covering the whole range of attitudes from enthusiasm to hostility. The statements must be short, and in simple terms, and should not be 'double-barrelled'. (A 'double-barrelled' statement has two parts—'Teaching is a worth-while job and offers good prospects of promotion'—where it is possible to agree with one part and disagree with the other.) Each statement is numbered and written on a card. A number of 'judges' (preferably twenty-five at least) are then asked to sort the cards into three piles, according to whether they think the statement expresses a favourable, neutral or hostile attitude. Each pile is then sorted into three smaller piles, giving nine categories in all—extremely favourable, favourable, moderately favourable; favourable-neutral, neutral, neutral-hostile; moderately hostile, hostile and extremely hostile. The identification numbers of the cards assigned to those categories by each judge are noted. For each item, a distribution of categories to which it has been assigned is then compiled. A 'good' item is one where there is close agreement among the judges about its position on the nine-point scale; but an item which is assigned to a wide range of categories must be discarded. The judges' decisions also provide a 'scale value' for the item: if four judges put statement 14 in category 6, twelve put it in category 7, and nine in category 8, the statement is a reasonably 'good' item, and has a scale value of 7·2, the median position. The attitudes of the judges themselves are irrelevant: their task is to interpret intelligently the implication of the statement.

The final stage in the construction of the scale is now to select about twenty to twenty-five statements, which are 'good' items and which also cover all nine points of the scale, without any large gaps between scale values. The statements are then arranged in random order. When the scale is applied, the subjects mark those statements with which they agree. For example, here are three statements from a Thurstone-type attitude scale on 'The Church'.

 1. I believe the church is a powerful agency for promoting both individual and social righteousness.          (1·3)
 2. I think the church is hundreds of years behind the times and cannot make a dent on modern life.          (6·5)
16. The churches may be doing a good and useful job, but they do not interest me.          (4·3)

A person completing this scale ticks the statements with which he agrees (or which are the closest approximation to his attitude). The scale values of the statements are given above in brackets, 1 being most favourable and 7 most hostile: these values do not, of course, appear on the scale. The attitude score is the median, or alternatively the mean, of the scale values of the statements marked.

The method described above is just one of various modifications in the original Thurstone scheme, but it is one which is widely used. The differences between methods lie mainly in the detailed organization of the various stages, not in the general principles.


LIKERT SCALE

While the Thurstone-type scale is still used in some investigations, the Likert-type scale makes fewer statistical assumptions and is probably the most widely used method of attitude measurement. Essentially the Likert scale again consists of a list of statements, but here the person answering is asked to make a judgement on *every* question or statement. For example, one such item might be 'It is important for me to do well at school'. The judgement may be simply 'Agree' or 'Disagree'; alternatively the degree of agreement may be indicated on a scale having up to say ten values. But it is difficult for most people to make such fine distinctions and scales with between three and six categories of response are normally preferable. A six-point scale might indicate the following degrees of agreement: strongly agree, definitely agree, probably agree, probably disagree, definitely disagree, strongly disagree. As with rating scales (see p. 122), the advantage of using an *even* number of response categories is that it is impossible to take refuge repeatedly in a completely 'neutral' category. On the other hand, 'don't know' or 'undecided' may be a necessary alternative answer to some questions, and then a scale with an *odd* number of categories may be preferred.

On the Likert-type scale the over-all attitude is measured by a score which is the sum of the weights given to each of the responses. The assignment of these weights is based on a previous standardization of the scale using a representative sample. The procedure for deciding weights is described by Edwards (1957, p. 149). Alternatively it may be sufficient to impose an arbitrary weighting system. For example, on a four-point scale a 3–2–1–0 weighting or scoring system may be found to be as useful as a more complicated method of calculating exact weights.

For example, Buxton's (1966) scale, designed to measure academic motivation, included statements such as:

1. I feel ashamed when I get a poor mark.
9. I think most homework is a bore.

Pupils marked each item as : . . . very true of me; . . . partly or usually true of me; . . . cannot say, no feeling one way or the other; . . . partly or usually *untrue* of me; . . . very *untrue* of me. For positive items, such as 1, the answer 'very true of me' was scored 5 and so on down to 1 for 'very *untrue* of me'. For a negative statement, such as 9, the scoring was reversed.

Before adding together the scores on each item of a Likert-type scale, it is important to check for internal consistency. A scale is not made just by gathering together a miscellaneous collection of items. The items in the inventory must each be assessing similar aspects—one item on anxiety cannot be added to one item on physical health, unless there is reason to believe that both are measuring the same dimension. To check this, a preliminary trial on a parallel sample is necessary, followed by an item analysis of the responses. The full-scale item analysis used for the standard personality inventories is seldom practicable, though any simplification of the full-scale procedure results in a loss of efficiency. The simplest method of pre-testing items for a short inventory to be included in some limited inquiry on a specific problem is the use of criterion groups. For example, if the investigation is to consider the relation of attitudes to performance in a school subject, the statements of attitudes are tested on pupils who can be classified into two groups, those who are known to be successful and those who are failing. Statements which discriminate between these two groups—which tend to be checked by the successful group and tend *not* to be checked by the unsuccessful group, or vice versa—can then be grouped together to form a short scale of relevant discriminating statements. (For attitude statements an index of discrimination of 15 per cent is usually accepted, compared with the 30 per cent required for items on intellectual tests; see the appendix to chapter 8.)

Other forms of item analysis measure internal consistency—the extent to which pupils who check one statement also tend to check the other statements—and these can also be used. However, unless the numbers involved in this preliminary trial of statements are fairly large, the results of a more complex item-analysis procedure may be invalid through the operation of chance factors.

OTHER ATTITUDE SCALES

A Guttman-type scale is a very short list of statements, but the construction is complex, involving 'scalogram analysis' (see Edwards, 1957, p. 172). Essentially it is a scale of as few as six or eight statements, each expressing a slightly different position on a scale of attitude, and the subject marks the one which most nearly expresses his attitude. Attitude to mathematics, for example, may range from '1. I hate maths' to '8. I like maths best of all subjects'.

In contrast, the method of paired comparisons involves a complicated presentation but is straightforward in principle. Thurstone's (1947) *Vocational Interest Schedule* uses this technique to assess attitudes to ten different types of occupation. Every possible pair among these ten types is listed, and the person completing the schedule makes a forced choice between each pair, recording a 'vote' in favour of one or other. The addition of the 'votes' lists the ten types of occupation in an order of preference. This method can be used to measure attitudes indirectly, through forced choices between alternative statements, or by asking for preferences between pairs of activities, or between pairs of school subjects. Buxton's research which was mentioned on p. 129, compared results from a Likert-type scale on academic motivation with results from a forced-choice scale, in which a pupil had to choose, in each of nineteen pairs of statements, the one which was 'more nearly true of him'—for example:

2*a*. I don't care much about my marks.
2*b*. I don't mind not having sport, if there is work to be done.

A series of ten attitude scales, constructed by the National Foundation for Educational Research for use with pupils aged 9 to 11 years, is described by Lunn (1969). The scales cover attitude to school, interest in school work, importance of doing well, attitude to the class, the image of the class as seen by others, the conforming or non-confirming pupil, relations with the teacher, anxiety about school work, social adjustment, and self-image. These scales were constructed in a series of stages, starting with group discussions with pupils and a pilot study on 355 children, followed by a factor analysis, a preliminary selection of items, application to 2,300 children, a further selection of items and finally application of a modified Guttman scalogram analysis. Few research projects will have the facilities to construct scales with this degree of thoroughness.

In chapters 4 and 5 it was suggested that short inventories and attitude scales could appropriately be included in an interview schedule or a questionnaire. Usually these will have to be constructed specifically for the project. For example, a questionnaire study investigating students' failure may seek to check the attitudes or study habits of students to see how these are related to success and failure. A group of statements may be run together into a short inventory section, to provide a more systematic study of one aspect of the problem. A single question merely divides the sample into those who check it and those who do not: the inventory with a number of items provides a scale of measurement. A Likert-type scale would be suitable for this use.

## CHECK LISTS

For some purposes, a check list is preferable to an inventory or attitude scale. In a check list, you mark or check only the items which apply. For example, the *Mooney Problem Check List*, College Form (1950) contains 330 items which cause anxiety to students. A student who seeks help or guidance is asked to mark the items which apply to him. A simple method of classification, explained in the manual, provides a basis for diagnosis of the area of difficulty. The check-list method has applications in a wide range of personality assessment, and its validity in any particular situation is tested in much the same way as an inventory. If an inquiry seeks to identify the qualities of a good teacher, a check list of qualities which appear to be relevant is prepared. This is tested on two groups of teachers, one agreed or assumed to be 'good teachers', the other 'poor teachers'. Clearly it is no use including items in the list which are checked equally for both groups: those items only are selected which discriminate between the groups. This is another example of a criterion group analysis which here will produce a scale suitable for application to student teachers. Stott's (1956) *Bristol Social Adjustment Guides* are examples of published check lists constructed by a technique of this kind.

This review of techniques of measurement has inevitably extended over the ill-defined border between attitudes and personality. The development of those methods has opened up possibilities of research into aspects of education which have often been neglected because they are not easy to study. However, there are certain weaknesses in this approach which must be noted.

The first points are statistical. Unless certain rigorous statistical tests have been applied, it cannot be assumed that items in a scale or inventory are equal units, to be added to give a total. Scores from inventories and attitude scales only provide a basis for ranking, and are not measures like height or temperature. In technical terms, the scores are on *ordinal* scales, not on *interval* scales. A score of 20 is not twice as extreme a result as a score of 10, just as a temperature of 20°C is not twice as warm as a temperature of 10°C. Also, not all units in a check list are necessarily of equal or even of similar importance. The combination of certain units which add to 20 may have a different significance from a score of 20 got from a different combination. In a check list of qualities of teachers, for example, an item such as 'speech defect' may be very rare but of overriding importance when it does occur. Again, one cannot assume that the importance of an item or aspect of inquiry applies equally over the whole range of the sample being studied. To illustrate this from the example of an inquiry into students' failure, consider the relevance of a quality such as anxiety. It may be that too little anxiety is as much a handicap to a student's progress as too much anxiety; or that anxiety is important only in combination with certain other factors, such as limited ability or faulty study habits. Special statistical methods may be required to bring out such relations in analysis. Even without such analysis, it is important to be aware of the general problem which these considerations raise with reference to the use of scales and inventories and check lists.

A final point is that all measurement involves the artificial isolation of one quality from a complex situation, and therefore fails to do justice to the uniqueness of individual events, objects or persons. 38–26–40 is a poor description of Venus de Milo, or indeed of any woman. But uniqueness is incompatible with comparison, evaluation and generalization, and measurement is necessary if personal judgements are to be tested against some independent or objective criterion.

SUMMARY

Attitudes are always specific to a certain context and hence attitude scales have a limited range of application. Different techniques of measuring attitudes include Thurstone-type and Likert-type scales, as well as check lists. Whatever technique is used, a pilot study is necessary to ensure that the scale is internally consistent. In addition validation through the analysis of the responses from criterion groups or from expert judges is a necessary part of developing an attitude scale. The scores obtained from such scales give a better indication of people's attitudes than a series of unconnected questions, but cannot be treated as if they were on interval scales. Such scores provide only an indication of the relative strengths of attitudes between different people.

| Observation and Case Studies

Previous chapters have described indirect methods of assessing people—inventories, scales, tests, questionnaire. Why not observe behaviour directly? The research worker busy over a calculating machine or feeding punched tape into a computer, is sometimes visited by a strange revelation, when he realizes that somewhere, almost in another world, there are real children, in classroom or playground, whose real behaviour must surely offer a bountiful source of information to test his theories or provide new insights. Certainly, it is important never to be so far from children that one forgets the setting of educational research. Some of the nonsense stemming from research studies which has often been written—but less often published—could only be written by someone who has spent too long away from the classroom. Contact with schools and with children is a necessary part of the work of research in education; but also a certain remoteness from the day-to-day work of schools may be necessary if we are to see the pattern behind the events, or to see the pattern in a new light.

Observation of children is a good starting point for research, but it takes us only a little way along the road to understanding. Observation must be to some purpose, if we are to see more than the kaleidoscope of events. Ideas and hypotheses are the framework of research, which observation fills out: without the theoretical framework, the data recorded are without shape or meaning.

## SYSTEMATIC OBSERVATION

In spite of certain difficulties, the direct observation of children's behaviour has a contribution to offer in research. One difficulty which can be readily overcome is the effect of the presence of an observer. Another much harder problem is the classifying of observations to provide a basis for comparison and analysis. In so far as one seeks to observe natural situations, as distinct from experimentally contrived situations, it follows that standard sequences of behaviour do not occur, and so each group of events is unique.

Technical developments have removed the need to have an observer present, taking notes. The one-way vision screen requires a double-glazed window, the glass on the observer's side being dark-tinted. If the observers sit in a dark room and the children's room is well lit, the observers are invisible. Holes in a panel which is painted white on the children's side, or a mirror with parts of the silvering removed, provide a cheap but much less adequate substitute in a small-scale experiment. Closed-circuit television equipment has made the one-way screen obsolescent. There is no need for a camera operator nor for sophisticated remote-control equipment: a fixed camera, set for wide-angle view and suspended from a corner of a room is quickly accepted and then ignored by the children. Video tape-recording, or cine-photography can be used to make a record which is available for detailed analysis, as well as providing a check on the reliability of classifications used, by replay to several 'judges'.

But a complete film of, say, a children's play session contains too much information. The use of time-sampling reduces the mass of information to a more manageable quantity. The appropriate form of time-sampling depends on the purpose of the observation. To measure variety of activity, the observer records what the children are doing in, say, the first minute in every five minutes over a period of any hour; or, to identify friendship groupings, he records which groups they are in once every fifteen or thirty minutes throughout the day. These sampling procedures are inappropriate if the aim is to record the frequency of changes of groups or the average length of time which different children spend in any one form of activity.

A much simpler procedure than any of these is based on a system of shorthand recording of selected actions, when the research is concerned only with certain types of behaviour. Provided there is a clearly defined hypothesis under test, a list of relevant actions can be prepared, and the occurrence of these, and these only, can be noted without the complications of mechanical recording and play-back.

In a formal classroom situation, when a new method of teaching is being tested, the proportion of time the pupils spend in various forms of activity can be recorded. Using symbols for, say, listening, answering, reading, individual work and daydreaming, one observer uses time-sampling to work round the class at a fixed rate, or several observers check individual pupils for longer periods, again on a sampling basis. If the aim is to examine different patterns of group work, the system of classification will include systematic work in a group, random movement among groups, working alone, and so on. These examples are over-simplified: a more adequate example can be given from the study of interaction within small groups. Observation of group inter-action not only provides insight into the social psychology of groups, but also is a means of assessing the personalities of the members of the group. Bales' Interaction Process Analysis (1950) is a system for assessment of this kind. The special attraction of this approach is that it is based on direct observation of personality in action in a social situation. Its difficulties, however, should not be under-rated, for the technique requires training and practice if it is to be used successfully.

McLeish (1968) described the system briefly:

'Interaction Process Analysis is a system devised by Dr R. F. Bales by which verbal and non-verbal 'acts' are coded and recorded by tallies in the appropriate 'category' for the individual making the act. There are twelve such categories (see below) chosen as appropriate by their economy and comprehensiveness as a system for describing behaviour. The tally also indicates to whom the act was directed, whether to another individual (and to which) or to the group as a whole. At the end of each observation period, the tallies are added and combined in various ways. For example, they provide detailed information about the total participation of each member (number of acts initiated and number of acts 'received'); the members to whom acts were addressed and by whom; the categories in which each member gave and received acts (i.e. what kind of statements he made, and what kind of reactions he received from other members); whether each member gave or received more acts in each category.

Since 1950, Bales has revised the content of some categories, so that the twelve categories in which 'acts' may be scored are now described as:

1. Seems friendly
2. Jokes or gives phantasy
3. Agrees
4. Gives suggestion
5. Gives opinion
6. Gives information
7. Asks for information or clarification
8. Asks for opinion
9. Asks for suggestion
10. Disagrees
11. Shows tension or laughs
12. Seems negative'

The question of whether or not auxiliaries should be employed to assist the teacher has led to increased interest in recording precisely the teacher's duties and activities throughout the school day. This also is essentially a problem of how to classify, how to record, and how to apply time-sampling. If the aim is to examine the proportion of time spent by a teacher in routine non-teaching duties, the categories employed for recording are very different from those needed for an inquiry to study the different roles a teacher performs in a day's work. This is an area of research in which we can expect to see a steady growth of interest, alongside the continuing concern with the systematic observation of pupil–pupil and pupil–teacher interactions. Much use is also made of the various approaches to mapping out the semi-permanent social structures which exist between children in the classroom.

## SOCIOMETRY

Sociometry is a technique for mapping the social structure of a group. But it is seldom applied to actual observation of grouping, relying instead on a questionnaire asking for declared preferences within a group or class of pupils. Each pupil nominates one or more persons whom he or she would choose as a friend, or to help in a project, or for one of a number of situations. Asking children who they would *not* choose, or who they dislike most, is usually discouraged by schools. From the preferences a chart of the bonds is drawn, and some pupils emerge as 'stars', having many lines between them and a wide range of pupils, while others show up as 'isolates'. The technique also identifies closed groups within a class, and can give a teacher an indication of a social structure within his class which he may not have realized. A full explanation is to be found in K. M. Evans' *Sociometry and Education* (1962). As a research technique, sociometry has the defect that, while it gives a good picture, its data are often difficult to analyse, especially if numbers are large. A straight count of the 'votes' received by each pupil is a starting point; but even this may be misleading in a survey covering several classes unless special care is taken to control the range of choice. Also, if each child is asked to nominate three friends, there is no way of knowing precisely the intensity of friendship in each choice. A simple count of number of choices, and a weighted total (3 for first choice, 2 for second, 1 for third) both involve unjustified assumptions. Since a decision on the appropriate method of statistical analysis is limited by the form of choice offered, the scoring procedure should be decided before the sociometric data are collected. Too many sociometry projects founder on a mass of information which has been too hastily gathered in a form which prevents an adequate analysis of the choices. The danger in a sociometric study, as with observational records, is that the information accumulates so rapidly. There is no merit in the mere gathering of information, however diligently and accurately it is recorded. There must be some purpose or theory or hypothesis to determine which pieces of information are relevant.

CASE STUDIES

Moving away from the social structures existing within groups, another promising area of study is the observation of individual children. This, of course, is the basis of clinical work with children, and the compiling of case studies is part of the training of a clinical psychologist. This alternative to survey or experimental work was mentioned in chapter 1. To draw up a detailed case study of one child, based on measurement and systematic observation, is a useful exercise for any person who has to work with children. A list of facts, however, or a record of what was said or done on various occasions, is only a starting point. Such work moves from anecdote to research only when there is a comprehensive interpretation, and interpretation is possible only when the data have been gathered according to a systematic plan. The classic example of research of this kind is the work of Piaget. Other studies on the model of his work have made important contributions to educational research. Donaldson (1963), for example, asked children to solve problems of the kind set in conventional intelligence tests, speaking aloud their thoughts so as to reveal the strategies they adopted and the errors they made. The sessions with each child were tape-recorded, and the analysis of the results revealed certain characteristic types of error which were made.

Observational data such as these can be given a wider frame of reference, if the data can be compared with some large-scale survey which has established norms for at least certain of the aspects studied with the small group. The *Bristol Social Adjustment Guides* mentioned in the previous chapter are examples of check lists of patterns of behaviour, covering the school, the home and the residential hostel. Certain forms of behaviour, they claim, are associated with characteristic personality traits, and comparison with these provides a framework for evaluation. Alternatively, various developmental scales are available, which have established age-norms for certain behaviour. Gesell's schedules, set out in a series of books, are among the best known of the developmental scales (*The First Five Years of Life. The Child from Five to Ten, Youth: The Years from Ten to Sixteen*). The *Vineland Social Maturity Scale* (Doll, 1947) lists 117 types of activity grouped according to the age at which these appear in the normal course of development. Unfortunately all Gesell's scales and the *Vineland Scales* are already out of date and have a marked American bias. An English version of the *Vineland Scale*, the *Manchester Scales of Social Adaptation* (Lunzer, 1966), is an extensive modification of the original: the manual shows the percentage of three age-groups (6–9, 9–12, 12–15) able to perform the listed activities.

The emphasis on statistics in many courses of training has given students the impression that only large-scale studies are 'real' research. There is clearly a place for the intensive study of a small sample, but at least two major weaknesses may be found in such 'depth' studies. It is difficult to generalize from a small sample which is often unrepresentative. Even if the sample has been selected at random, and the results are statistically significant, a conclusion based on, say, ten cases tends to be regarded as suspect. Whatever statisticians may deduce from the abstract world of probability theory, events usually show that these doubts are justified. In educational research, where there are many interacting variables in even the simplest study, it is almost impossible to ensure that a small sample is representative in all respects— though this is what the statisticians must assume. The solution is not necessarily to insist on large numbers, but to replicate small-scale experiments—that is, to repeat them with another small group under identical conditions to see if the same conclusions emerge. Too often, a research worker falls into the trap of formulating his hypotheses after he has seen what his data suggest, and this false procedure gives spurious statistical respectability to the 1 in 100 chance result. The other weakness of individual studies is linked with a related point. The strength of this procedure is that it enables the research worker to take full account of the uniqueness of each individual, and for that very reason it is difficult to reconcile the procedure with the demands of experimental requirements. This is a point which has been discussed in an earlier chapter (chapter 10). Its implication here is that individual studies are often most effective in the early stages of research, for an exploratory role, to open up a new area of investigation, to challenge old assumptions and suggest new insights. The pains-taking labour of confirming these hints and suggestions is likely to require a more systematic style of inquiry in a less personal form.

The reader who has patiently followed the development of a large variety of different measurement techniques which started in chapter 4, has now come full circle. In the last paragraph the importance of systematic inquiry in educational research was stressed—and this requires careful planning. In chapter 2 we laid out seven stages in planning a research project. After the initial stages of deciding on the topic and defining the sample, the research worker chooses his method of measurement. The guide-lines which have been presented in nine out of the preceding ten chapters should help with this selection. We have already discussed how the data can be condensed into tabular form, though the essential problem of testing the statistical significance of the results has been side-stepped. There remain the two important stages of interpreting the results and writing the report. But before returning to that final coda, there is a chapter on curriculum development—a cadenza perhaps? In spite of all the emphasis on precise measurement which has marked much of the previous discussion, it is important to recognize an area of educational innovation in which quantitative evaluation is un-common. The following chapter does not fit easily into any of the categories of research, but it describes an area of activity which may be seen to have a direct and immediate impact on what happens in the classroom.

SUMMARY

Systematic observation of children, by use of video tape-recording techniques backed up by methods of time-sampling and observa-tion schedules, has led to complex analysis of the interactions between pupils and between teacher and pupils. The social structures which exist within the classroom can be mapped out through investigations using sociometry. Individual case studies can provide detailed information about the development of particular children. Large-scale studies have provided normative scales of development against which the relative maturity of individual children can be compared.

Interest in curricular change is not new. In 1922 Sir John Adams wrote *Modern Developments in Educational Practice* in which there was a strong plea for reform from Caldwell Cook. 'The educational system has, in fact, not been evolving at all, it has been congealing. And now it has become clogged, stuck fast' (p. 18). Adams described the educational developments of the early twentieth century. Educational experiments were numerous, if not wide-spread: the Dalton Plan, the Gary System, the Play Way and the Project Method were all making their contribution towards changing teaching methods. Their combined effects can be seen in many present-day primary schools and yet it is only compar-atively recently that curriculum development has become dominant in educational research activity. Previously attempts to inject new ideas into the educational system had been left to enthusiastic individuals, and as a result the 'new education' made little impression on the majority of schools. The present activity in curricular reform is different in at least two important ways. It has become more systematic in approach and it is also better organized. The enthusiasts are beginning to analyse their activities more critically and, through the Schools Council, they have found channels of communication which reach many other practising teachers.

## THE SYSTEMATIC APPROACH

The first major attempts at curriculum development were mounted in the United States about the time when America entered the 'space race'. Public interest stimulated a critical analysis of scientific education in the United States, backed by huge financial outlays. Universities and schools co-operated in developing not only new syllabuses but also new textbooks, teachers' guides, films and apparatus. One of the main aims of these schemes was to bring the school syllabuses more into line with current scientific developments. In England the syllabuses in scientific subjects were similarly antique. Even in 1960 the A-level Physics syllabuses of several examination boards contained little mention of twentieth-century advances in the subject. Atomic physics was barely hinted at and by the time 'electronic valves' had crept into a corner of the syllabus, transistors had virtually replaced them in electronic equipment. In such rapidly developing disciplines, the need for curriculum development is obvious.

The Nuffield Science and Mathematics Projects have set the pace and, to some extent, determined the pattern of later projects. The systematic approach used in these projects is essentially pragmatic. The research is run by a working party consisting of teachers and college or university lecturers in the particular subject specialism. Their aim is to modernize the syllabus and present this body of knowledge to pupils in an interesting way by developing more appropriate methods of presentation. For the Nuffield schemes the emphasis was on using practical work to involve the pupils in 'discovery' methods of learning and hence to increase their understanding of the subject. In Bulletin No. 1 of the Nuffield Mathematics Project, the starting point was seen as the attempt to produce:

'a contemporary course for children from 5–13. This will be designed to help them to connect together many aspects of the world about them, to introduce them gradually to the processes of abstract thinking, and to foster in them a critical, logical, but also creative, turn of mind. . . . A synthesis will be made of what is worth preserving in the traditional work with various new ideas, some of which are already being tried out. These cover presentation as well as content, and emphasis will be placed on the learning process: sleight of hand will not pass as a substitute for genuine understanding. A concrete approach will be made to abstract concepts, and the children will make their own discoveries whenever possible. The work of the project will be set against the present background of new thinking concerning mathematics itself' (Matthews, 1964).

This passage sums up admirably the characteristics of many similar projects in curriculum development. There is a careful indication of the aims of the new approaches to teaching, and high in the priorities come the modernization of the syllabuses and a greater emphasis on children's understanding as opposed to simply knowledge or skill. In presenting the syllabus teachers are expected to relate the knowledge and ideas to the real world and to the experience of the pupil. It is assumed that children should be expected to reach abstract conceptions through 'discovery' or practical experience.

The Nuffield projects not only set about revising the syllabuses; they also produced curriculum 'packages'. It was realized that one of the reasons for the slowness of change in the scientific subjects was the very real problems facing teachers in the classroom. There was no time to start developing new materials with which to emphasize the 'discovery' approach; widespread adoption of these new ideas necessitated the provision of ready-made curriculum packages. In science subjects new experiments were designed and, in mathematics, apparatus was produced to provide concrete examples of mathematical concepts. Teachers' guides were published to explain how to use the 'packages' and, in the early stages, volunteer schools tried out the new syllabuses and materials.

After many trials, the teachers reported to the working parties the advantages and disadvantages of both syllabuses and materials. By a process of trial and error and evaluation by consensus of opinion the final published form of the teachers' guides and materials was reached. This approach to curriculum development, systematic if not scientific, has been widely applied.

The Schools Council Working Paper No. 10 (1967*a*) lists the 'essential elements' in curriculum development as:

1. Definition of aims and objectives.
2. Selection of appropriate content, methods and materials.
3. Evaluation of the extent to which the new approaches achieve the defined objectives.
4. Feedback of results to teachers leading to further development.

These four stages have been treated in different ways by different projects, but they represent a commonly accepted pattern. Taking these stages separately, it will be possible to describe in more detail the research methods which are being used in curriculum development.

AIMS AND OBJECTIVES

The influence of the linguistic philosophers is obvious here. In the past educationists have been allowed to use woolly clinhés to describe their aims. Under the scrutiny of philosophers such as Peters and Hirst, a concern for greater conceptual clarity has been growing. The curriculum itself must be defined. Taylor (1966) has indicated that the traditional view of the curriculum, as 'a grouping of subjects for study', is now too restricted a definition. He prefers a psychologically oriented definition which relates the curriculum to the 'learning experiences' of the pupils. Taken more broadly still it is possible to take the curriculum to include everything within the school environment which may affect the efficiency of the pupils' learning (Neagley and Evans, 1967). In this way the curriculum embraces not only the content of the syllabuses, the teaching methods, the materials—books, audio-visual aids, teaching machines, but also the way in which the school is organized—streaming, setting, team-teaching—and even the architectural design of the school buildings. All these components within a school may influence learning and are considered under the heading of the curriculum.

One result of the current interest in curricular reform has been the new approach to aims and objectives. Philosophers were wont to speak in broad general terms about educational aims in their discussions about what should be taught in schools. The impact of these idealistic views on the schools was negligible. More recently the Newsom Report (Ministry of Education, 1963) tried to identify current educational aims in the context of pupils of average or less than average ability.

'Boys and girls need to be helped to develop certain skills of communication in speech and in writing, in reading with understanding and in calculations involving numbers and measurement: ... [they] need to develop, as well as skills, capacities for thought, judgement, enjoyment, curiosity. They need to develop a sense of responsibility for their work and towards other people, and to begin to arrive at some code of moral and social behaviour which is self-imposed' (paragraph 76).

The difficulty in implementing such aims stems from their generality. What content, methods or materials should be used to achieve these important aims? Teachers get little guidance from vague ideals. There is a great need to be more precise and to introduce what Kerr (1968) has called 'curriculum objectives', as distinct from the more general 'educational aims'. Psychologists of the behaviourist school demand that the objectives used in education should be defined in behavioural terms. In other words, the teacher should specify at the beginning of the course in what ways his students' behaviour will differ at the end of the course; he must then measure that 'terminal behaviour'. Only in this way can the teacher be sure of the efficacy of his teaching methods.

If objectives are to be stated in operational or behavioural terms it is important to analyse the processes commonly involved in various types of education. In the United States a hierarchical arrangement (taxonomy) of educational objectives has been evolved by Bloom (1956) and Krathwohl (1964). These two handbooks deal with the 'cognitive' and 'affective' domains of behaviour: a further domain, that of 'psycho-motor skills', has yet to be developed. Within the cognitive and affective domains, Bloom and his co-workers have produced the following sub-divisions.

| Cognitive domain | Affective domain |
|---|---|
| Knowledge | Receiving or attending |
| Comprehension | Responding |
| Application | Valuing |
| Analysis | Organization of value system |
| Synthesis | Generalization or characterization |
| Evaluation | of value system |

The application of Bloom's taxonomies has helped many research workers to decide on the specific objectives within different subjects. It certainly forces the teacher to look beyond the syllabus to the specific changes in knowledge, comprehension and analysis required of his pupils by the end of the course.

One great advantage of this approach to curriculum development is that it sets up objectives which can be evaluated in terms of specific changes in behaviour. A serious limitation is the underlying assumption that the curriculum is no more than the sum total of a series of measurable elements. Breaking down educational aims into behavioural 'atoms' carries with it the danger of concentrating exclusively on the aspects of the curriculum which can most readily be assessed. Many teachers, especially those of the 'humanities', have rejected this atomistic view of curriculum objectives, in favour of more general aims. But even if broad educational aims are used to direct curriculum development, some form of evaluation must follow. But here the changes in behaviour are analysed in retrospect, in an attempt to decide which specific gains have been made during the course. These gains in, for example, knowledge or attitudes are then compared with the original aims of the course.

## CONTENT, METHODS AND MATERIALS

The Nuffield approach to this stage has already been outlined. After pilot trials the curriculum 'packages'—textbooks, teachers' guides and apparatus—are tried out in widespread 'field trials'. In other subject areas similar approaches have been used. The

Schools Council have published details of how teachers may best tackle the problems associated with raising the school leaving age. Essentially these schemes tackle subject areas such as science, languages or the humanities. For each area it is possible to devise methods and materials which are of more immediate interest to 'Newsom' pupils. Common approaches are again apparent; for example, the curriculum is more outward looking. Typically a scheme would be built around a project such as 'communication' or 'transport' (see *Society and the Young School Leaver*, Schools Council, 1967b). Careful planning would provide a series of varied learning experiences. The topic of 'communication' might start with a visit from the local newspaper editor talking to the whole year-group, followed by a film about the newspaper industry. Such events provide the stimulus from which the project develops. Discussions in small groups might follow, leading to individual projects directed through 'work-cards' which suggest lines of inquiry about related topics.

The key to the success of such integrated approaches to learning seems to be the involvement of pupils in the local community and the careful preparation by the teachers of the individual assignments.

The decisions in grouping taken in curriculum projects of this kind seem, on occasions, to be contradictory. There is a tendency to use at one time large groups taught by lecture, film or television and to prefer at other times individual or small-group instruction. But this appears contradictory only in terms of the underlying assumption of the present educational system that teaching is always most effective in groups of thirty to forty children. The work of psychologists such as Gagné (1967) suggests that different conditions of learning should be provided for different purposes. At present the use of large groups or small groups is not linked closely with any theory of the curriculum. We do not yet know exactly what type of learning should take place in what size of group. It seems reasonable that films or lectures should be presented to large groups and that these also serve as an initial stimulus or focus of interest from which to develop a project. Discussions may well be most useful for changing attitudes. But under what conditions are individual assignments or programmed learning most effective? And what particular skills or attitudes of mind do they develop compared with classroom instruction? It seems important that those responsible for developing curricula should look towards the disciplines of philosophy and psychology for clarification of their ideas. The philosopher is often able to point towards certain fundamental relations between subject areas (Hirst, 1965) and the psychologists, in certain limited ways, can suggest profitable approaches towards improving the efficiency of learning (Cronbach, 1964*b*). For a fuller discussion of the contributions of these and other disciplines to curriculum development, the reader is referred to the papers brought together by Kerr (1968) under the title of *Changing the Curriculum*.

EVALUATION

In Nuffield and Schools Council projects, evaluation is generally through a consensus of teachers' opinions. Groups of experienced teachers are used to look for examples of current 'best practice' already being used in the schools. The curriculum packages developed in this way represent an amalgam of different approaches, all of which have been seen to work in practice. The weakness of this method of evaluation is apparent. The enthusiasts who develop new techniques of teaching *know* that their methods work. The methods work for them, but would they work for others or in a different setting? The brilliant teacher can probably make most methods appear to be successful: the dispirited teacher can make the best scheme appear dull. On the other hand, if a method has been tried out by many teachers in a variety of different schools, the consensus verdict is useful; but it is still a long way from scientific evaluation.

The research worker is more interested to know whether the precise objectives of the course have been achieved. He requires quantified evidence about the 'learning outcomes' and an indication of which *parts* of the schemes have been responsible for the particular changes in behaviour noticed. And quantitative evaluation demands accurate measures. In chapter 8 various methods of measuring attainment were mentioned, but these are most suitable for examining 'knowledge' and 'comprehension'. Modern curricula generally are aimed at developing higher order skills—'a critical, logical, but also creative, turn of mind'. These are less easily measured by traditional attainment tests, and measures of creativity or divergent thinking, which were mentioned in chapter 10, are still at the experimental stage. Beyond the 'cognitive domain', many teachers are also interested in developing positive attitudes towards learning and in providing for future leisure interests. It is even more difficult to assess the efficacy of teaching methods in achieving these ends.

Until a greater variety of measurement instruments is available, it seems probable that curriculum development cannot be scientific in its approaches. It will continue to rely heavily on the intuitive assessments of experienced teachers. But if teachers' reports are to be of value, they must be more than just a general expression in favour of or against the innovations. For example, a class teacher can gather relevant and quite detailed information from open-ended questions to the class or from discussion in which pupils bring out their feelings toward, or understanding of, certain ideas or attitudes which the teaching has aimed to develop. It is essential that such questions be 'sufficiently unstructured not to cue the pupils as to what response might be expected' (Rudd, 1969). Records, systematically collected, of pupils' leisure activities or of their writing (for example, using the essay procedure described in chapter 10), or direct observation of their behaviour (using the techniques described in chapter 13), can also provide useful information which can be worked into a larger-scale evaluation of a new approach or syllabus. Contrived situations can also be used as part of evaluation, such as the discussion of unfinished stories or incidents (as in the projective techniques described in chapter 10), following up with questions, 'Why did these things happen?' 'How did those involved feel?' 'What would you do in this situation?' and so on. Evaluation in curriculum development may thus include many of the techniques which have been described in previous chapters.

FEEDBACK OF RESULTS

In a rapidly developing society, this final stage in curriculum development is crucial. Unless the results are fed back into the system rapidly and widely, the mainstream of education will not benefit. It must be the majority, not the minority, of teachers who adopt the new approaches, and curriculum change must be a *continuing process* if it is to keep pace with a rapidly changing society. In England the need to centralize the process of reforming the curriculum led in 1962 to the setting up of the Curriculum Study Group in the Ministry of Education. Teachers' representatives objected to the possibility of governmental control of curricula and in 1964 the Schools Council was formed. This body represents teachers, universities, colleges, local education authorities and the Department of Education and Science, but teachers have the predominant influence. The Schools Council has encouraged local education authorities to set up teachers' centres to stimulate co-operative effort in curriculum development projects. Through these local groups and through a series of 'Working Papers' the Schools Council has attempted to disseminate the results of its many projects. Curriculum Bulletins are also being prepared as guides for teachers. Full details of these publications can be obtained from H.M. Stationery Office. A description of the projects sponsored by the Schools Council is given in the Council's report, *The First Three Years* (1968b). But the projects themselves cannot be useful unless the results are accepted by the vast majority of teachers. It is through the involvement of teachers in the local centres, developing and testing new curricula in the schools, that new approaches to teaching are most likely to be successful. Wide discussion of the results also stimulates further ideas and ensures continuing evolution of the curriculum.


CURRICULUM DEVELOPMENT IN SCOTLAND

The pattern of curriculum which has been described so far is that which has evolved in the work of the Nuffield Foundation and the Schools Council. In Scotland the procedure has been organized centrally. Working groups of teachers have been set up, each with a specific remit. For example, the Mathematics Syllabus Committee, set up in 1963, consisted of fifteen mathematics teachers, two college of education lecturers and four inspectors, and three university lecturers joined the committee soon after. The Committee drafted and tested new syllabuses, and on the basis of experimental trials in a group of sixty schools produced a series of nine textbooks, *Modern Mathematics in Schools* (see Robertson, 1969). The co-ordinating body is the Consultative Committee on the Curriculum, a committee of the Scottish Education Department, which at present has twelve such groups at work on different aspects of the curriculum. A description is given in the Committee's *First Report* (Scottish Education Department, 1969).

EXPERIMENTAL METHOD IN CURRICULUM DEVELOPMENT

While the activities of these national organizations have dominated the scene in curriculum development in recent years, numerous more specific studies have been carried out on aspects of curriculum construction. Word frequency counts, for example, have been made in many European and some Asiatic languages, and these have contributed to determining the appropriate content of a curriculum of study in the learning of foreign languages, in compiling spelling lists and in selecting the vocabulary for infant readers. Frequency counts have also been used as a basis for calculating an objective 'readability formula'. There are other possible uses of this technique, such as counting the various number combinations exercised in the examples set in arithmetic textbooks to ensure a balanced coverage, or checking the frequences of various kinds of error commonly made by children at different ages and stages to identify 'accident zones' where special care is needed. A review of recent research on frequency counts is given by Nisbet (1960).

Programmed learning is another area of research particularly relevant to curriculum development. Leith's *A Handbook of Programmed Learning* (1966) is one of several books which summarize work in this field. Evaluation is an integral element in the construction of programs, and the effect of different methods of programmed learning have been studied in many investigations using the experimental design described in chapter 1. Such a design might appear to be ideal generally for the evaluation of new curricula. Comparing the results of matched 'experimental' and 'control' groups being taught in modern and traditional ways would seem to offer the most satisfactory method of deciding between the two approaches. But the difficulty in obtaining tests which are appropriate to the objectives of *both* teaching methods has proved a stumbling block. One major project in Britain which used this approach was Downing's (1967) evaluation of i.t.a. The NFER have more recently reported a similar approach to assessing the contribution of the study of French in the primary school (Burstall, 1968).

Downing set out to compare the rates at which children learned to read using the initial teaching alphabet (i.t.a.) and traditional orthography (t.o.). For this purpose he designed an experiment in which groups of children throughout the country were taught either by i.t.a. or t.o. This study illustrates many of the points made earlier in this book. Downing obtained a representative sample of children by three-stage sampling. He sampled first schools, then teachers within schools, and finally children within classes. The groups were matched on seven background variables, such as size of school and amenities within the school building, and on four pupil variables: intelligence, social class, age and sex. Downing was able to show that there were few significant differences between the groups, which could thus be considered comparable for most of his purposes. The experimental group was taught to read through i.t.a.; the control group was taught through t.o. At the end of the third year, the experimental group had significantly higher mean scores on all the reading tests presented in t.o. These tests included word recognition, accuracy, speed and comprehension.

This would appear to be the sort of proof that would lead to wide acceptance. But although Downing's study has been one of the few to attempt to evaluate curriculum development in a scientific manner, the results have not been widely accepted. The criticisms of this experiment illustrate the difficulty of proving causal relations in education. Were the gains shown by the experimental group really the *result* of using i.t.a.? Downing's critics have been quick to point out other possibilities. The superiority of the experimental group might be caused by such factors as the 'Hawthorne effect' (see Downing, 1967, p. 6), the new i.t.a. books provided, the method of statistical analysis, and the greater degree of involvement felt by teachers using i.t.a. While these possibilities do exist, the project certainly made a real attempt to evaluate in an objective scientific manner the success of using i.t.a. The criticism used to question Downing's results may be equally applicable to a large number of other curriculum development projects. The effect of teachers' involvement in new schemes of work may well go a long way towards ensuring the apparent success of almost any method in its early days. Other projects, which used less rigorous attempts to evaluate the outcomes, have escaped these criticisms.

SUMMARY

Curriculum is taken to be any part of the school environment which may affect learning. Curriculum development can thus involve changing subject content, apparatus, organization, school architecture or methods of teaching. Advances in curriculum design are likely to become more effective through a more systematic approach. Educational objectives are carefully defined; content, method and materials are then chosen so as to achieve these ends. The success of the new schemes is evaluated—ideally by experimental comparisons—but more often by a concensus of teachers' opinions. Feedback of the results to the main body of teachers ensures that curriculum development becomes a cyclical process, keeping pace with a rapidly developing society.

| Interpreting Results

Various pitfalls in the use of research techniques and common errors in their interpretation have been mentioned in previous chapters. Hawthorne and halo effects are only two of many distorting influences on results. Sampling is a common source of bias, especially 'self-sampling', as when a questionnaire is returned only by those who hold strong views on a topic, or when teachers volunteer to use a new method and non-volunteers constitute a control group. In personality inventories, people check those responses which they think socially acceptable. Children are liable to treat all questions as some kind of test, and set themselves to discover what is the 'right' answer'. The choice of tests for a research project is particularly crucial: some of the important considerations are listed in chapter 8. Results can so often be explained away as specific to one particular test used that it is advisable to 'double bank' on important evaluation measures. If results from two tests are consistent, this is much more convincing, especially if the tests use different styles of approach. The previous chapter mentioned some of the complications which can arise in interpreting results, using the example of the i.t.a. study by Downing. The criticisms set out in *The i.t.a. Symposium* (Downing, 1967) explain how even a carefully planned large-scale experiment can produce results which are still the subject of controversy.

In addition to the technical points already mentioned, there are also important points of logic, such as the *post hoc ergo propter hoc* fallacy. We reduce the amount of time spent on spelling, and children's spelling improves. What does this prove? Confusion of correlation and cause—equating a significant association with a causal link—is a common example of this fallacy. Students who smoke tend to get poorer marks in examinations than nonsmokers. Students who sit in the front seats tend to get higher marks than those who sit in the back seats. Children who have to travel long distances to school tend to show more anxiety than those who live near the school. Does smoking dull the mind? Can you improve your chance of passing an examination by sitting nearer the front? Is it a mistake to close small rural schools?

These problems of interpretation arise when an association or a difference is shown to be statistically significant. On the other hand, the finding that the association or difference is *not* statistically significant does not justify a conclusion that no association exists or that two groups are the same. The failure of a result to reach statistical significance merely implies that the findings *may* be the product of chance factors in the sampling. Non-significant findings may also result because a sample is too small, or because the measures used are not sufficiently reliable or valid to show up whatever differences exist. Also, two groups may fail to show a significant difference because the relevant measure was not applied.

With the introduction of computers, research studies can now review the association of many variables simultaneously, and it is quite common for a computer to be used to check several hundred associations to identify significant results. In a wide-ranging sweep of this kind, five in every hundred checks will show *by chance alone* a significant result (at the 5 per cent level). On a smaller scale, the same principle applies. A teacher or student, examining data in a small-scale research study, may notice an unusual finding. He applies a statistical test and discovers that it is a significant result. In fact, in reviewing the data, he may have turned over in his mind at least twenty possible manipulations in his data, only to dismiss nineteen of these as inconclusive: the twentieth proves significant at the 5 per cent level. A result of this kind, discovered *after* the data are to hand, must be tested on a new sample. Otherwise we are thinking at the level of the child who has a 'lucky' penny which always comes up heads— or at least it once came up heads ten times in succession. A member of Aberdeen University staff in the 1940s noticed that a high proportion of his male colleagues parted their hair on the right, whereas most men part their hair on the left. A statistical test showed that the odds against his observation being a chance result were about a million to one. Is this, then, a physical sign of academic ability? He waited for twenty years and checked the finding on a new generation of university teachers. The hair-parting distribution in this group was identical to that of the adult male population.

The most difficult problems of interpretation arise when complex statistical processes are used for analysis of data. This book has not attempted to describe statistical methods—there are many other texts available. But most statistics texts lay such stress on the mathematics and computation of the various procedures that they gloss over or omit the equally difficult question of the meaning and interpretation of results. The point is illustrated in the remainder of this chapter by a scrutiny of one pattern of research design—the follow-up study.

If tests or examinations are used in selection or guidance, their validity for such a purpose should be checked by following up a group of pupils. If performance in the tests or examinations agrees closely with performance in the course for which they have been selected, this is evidence of predictive validity. The validity of 11-plus selection was tested by many such follow-up studies into secondary school. Even when 11-plus selection is replaced by guidance, it is necessary to know the predictive validity of assessments if sound advice is to be given. Should headmasters' estimates be taken into account in selection for higher education? A follow-up study of an intake into university compares GCE performance with final degree examination results, and then tests whether the headmasters' estimates can add effect-ively to the accuracy of prediction. A pupil wishes to study shorthand: is there any means by which we can predict whether or not she is likely to be successful? There are tests which carry the title 'Stenographic Aptitude Tests', but before we place too much reliance on these, we must know their predictive validity, and this requires a follow-up study. We can seldom hope that a single test will give all the information we require for adequate guidance: normally we base our judgement on a range of varied assessments. In the research design, the range of initial assessments is called the test battery (though it may include items which are not strictly tests). The validity of the test battery is established by comparison with a criterion of final performance. The best prediction of this criterion is usually obtained by giving different weights to the scores obtained in the various tests in the battery. The statistical technique for calculating these 'best weights' is known as multiple regression.

However much we may object to the idea of selection, this procedure for testing the validity of assessments is a necessary part of any system in which there is a choice to be made, whether it is a choice made by the individual or a selection process in which some other person makes the choice. The procedure has helped to improve both guidance and selection, and could be applied with advantage in many areas of education where un-tested procedures, such as interviews, are widely relied on. However, a few examples will demonstrate the complexities in this apparently straightforward experimental design.

A study of the prediction of success in shorthand, for example, reveals that a spelling test is the best single predictor. A follow-up study of engineering students shows the G C E English mark is the best predictor. A war-time inquiry into the selection of army cooks identifies a vocabulary test as the best predictor of success. How are we to interpret such findings? In all three cases, the explanation is that the criterion is faulty. The criterion in the shorthand course is a test of transcription of a passage, in which spelling errors are heavily penalized. Since the actual passage is well within the shorthand ability of the candidates, the ranking on the test is essentially in order of competence in spelling, and, not surprisingly, a spelling test predicts this order more accurately than any other. The engineering students are judged on their final examinations, which are of the essay type: the result of the follow-up study points to defects in this criterion. The army cooks, at the end of their course of training, are required to sit a three-stage examination: to prepare a specimen menu for a week, to cook a specimen meal, and to write an essay on the subject, 'An army marches on its stomach'. All the cooks have learned their specimen menu off by heart, and assessment of the meal is so subjective that it totally lacks reliability and validity. When marks in the final examination are added up, the essay mark (together with random influences) determines the order of merit. When this final order of merit is compared with the scores in the tests which had been given to the recruits before selection for training as cooks, it appears that the vocabulary test is the best at picking out the good cooks. In fact, it merely picks out those who do well in the examination at the end of the cooks' training; but this examination is not a valid criterion. The problem of establishing a sound criterion, and of guarding against a misleading one, is also the most serious obstacle to research in selection for university entrance and teacher training.

The need for choosing an *appropriate criterion* is not limited to follow-up studies in higher education or in the army. Many studies in schools have investigated the relation between various personality, attitudinal or intellectual measures and attainment. But how is attainment to be assessed? This is the criterion and the key measurement in these studies. One study shows a negative relation between 'extraversion' and 'attainment'; another study may come up with a positive relation. Unless the same test of extraversion and the same type of measure of attainment have been used, it is not surprising if the results differ. Attainment usually implies to teachers the total examination marks or total term marks in all subjects. The research worker would insist that these should be scaled against a standard test before use. But some research studies have measured attainment as the result of a single test or as the scores on the 'post-test' following a programmed learning session. The factors which influence learning from teaching machines over a series of, say, twenty thirty-minute sessions may well be different from those operating in the class-room over all subjects and throughout the whole term.

One important recent study into the relations between a number of social variables and attainment in the primary school (Plowden Report, 1967, volume 2, appendix 4) has been widely quoted. An elegant and complex step-regression analysis produced evidence of the relations between parental interest and attainment.

The implications are spelt out in detail in volume 1 of the Plowden Report. But the criterion of attainment used was one of two reading tests; and thus the whole argument rests on a score derived over a short period of time and on a single skill. Reading is of crucial importance in primary schools, but a score on a reading test is hardly 'primary school attainment'. Reading is probably more closely related to parental interest than computational skill would be. The results are thus immediately biased by the use of this criterion; a fact that is perhaps not sufficiently emphasized in discussions of the implications.

A second source of error is the *self-fulfilling prophecy*. When the test battery is used to select only a limited number of candidates who go forward into the course, while the remainder are directed into a lower-grade course, a criterion which covers the whole range of candidates will show a spuriously high agreement with the test battery. For only those who have high scores in the battery can qualify for the highest grades in the criterion. In selection for secondary education, an additional influence may operate. If high scorers at 11-plus receive better instruction in an atmosphere of success and high expectation, and the opposite applies to low scorers, it is not surprising if the prophecy is self-fulfilling.

However, a quite different complication arises if the follow-up is restricted to only the successful candidates. The range of performance in the test battery is reduced drastically, since only those above a certain level are admitted. This *attenuation through homogeneity*, as it is called, diminishes the correlation between test battery and criterion equally drastically. The point can be illustrated by an analogy. A hundred applicants wish to train as pilots, but only the best ten on selection tests are admitted to training. If all the hundred had undergone training, these ten would probably emerge quite high in the final assessment, thus demonstrating a reasonable correlation between test battery and criterion. But among the ten alone, there is likely to be a considerable rearrangement in rank order, and it is much less likely that the same person will be best in both the selection tests and the final assessment.

Unfortunately, this attenuation applies only to tests which constitute the basis of selection, or to tests which are correlated with the test battery. If a new and quite unrelated test is introduced—say, a test of manipulating geometric designs—and the validity of this new test is measured by a follow-up of the selected group only, the attenuation through homogeneity affects the selection tests only and the validity of the new test is spuriously enhanced.

This process of attenuation affects correlation. If, instead, we try to use average score on some index of performance, we encounter a different statistical complication, that of regression. A group of backward pupils is identified by taking those who score below 80 on a reading test. After a period of remedial instruction, the same test is repeated. Their average score has increased. Had we taken a group whose scores were above 120 (assuming 100 to be an average score), the probable result is a decrease on re-testing. Since the rank order is not identical on every occasion of testing, choosing the lowest group on one occasion means that some are bound to rise on the second occasion. If we choose the best five pupils, they can only hold their position or drop back in ranking. Certainly, they can improve their actual score, but the tendency is towards *regression to the mean*. If a group of men over six feet in height is chosen, the average mature height of their sons will be only about five feet ten inches—above average, but not as much above as their fathers. If a group of sons over six feet is chosen, the average height of their fathers will be only about five feet ten inches. In each case there is regression to the mean.

The characteristics of over-achievers and under-achievers have been investigated in many studies, but regression to the mean again clouds the interpretation of the results. If over-achievement is defined as those pupils whose attainment scores are 10 points more than their verbal reasoning scores, and under-achievement is defined similarly, it is possible to form two groups of children—the over-achievers and the under-achievers. But the two groups will be different in one important way. The over-achievers as a group will have a lower mean verbal reasoning score than the under-achievers. The cause is regression to the mean. The children who have the lowest scores cannot be under-achievers. And the resulting difference in intelligence between the groups may prevent any meaningful comparisons. The effect of regression to the mean is widespread and all too often goes unrecognized.

There are further statistical complications in the follow-up design to test the validity of selection and guidance procedures. The technique of multiple regression was mentioned earlier as the procedure by which the 'best weights' are calculated for the test battery. The more complex the statistical procedure, the greater is the danger of faulty interpretation. Multiple regression may produce odd results if two very similar tests are included in the battery and if by chance one of these tests has a higher correlation with the criterion than the other. As a result of this chance difference, one test may receive a much boosted weighting, and the other a negative weight. Sampling errors may also produce the effect of a spuriously high predictive value for the weighted test battery. The optimum weights are calculated from the data of the follow-up study. If the same data are then used to calculate the predictive value of the weighted battery (the multiple correlation of battery and criterion), the chance errors are counted in twice instead of being excluded. To avoid this, the follow-up sample should be large enough to allow all calculations to be done separately on two halves, and the weights derived from one half are applied to the data from the other half to produce an accurate estimate of prediction. This process of *cross-validation* on different samples from the same population is of great importance in educational research.

These points perhaps merely demonstrate that it is dangerous to play with statistical analysis. The advent of computers has increased the danger of the use of complex statistical analysis by people who do not thoroughly understand their limitations. But probably the most serious misuse of research findings is to be found in the way the implications from results are extended beyond the population on which the study was done and also into quite different educational situations. This process of extrapolation beyond the limits of the original study is hazardous.

Where the situations appear sufficiently similar or where the results from a complementary series of studies appear to justify extending the implications, it may be acceptable. But it should always be made clear in the discussion of the results at what stage the implications go beyond the findings. There is a place for conjecture, if it stimulates further research or innovation in the classroom, but at some stage it is important to repeat the study under appropriate conditions to test whether the conjecture has been justified.

A further danger in the use of research findings was discussed in chapter 8. It bears repeating as a final warning. The study by Kirkwood (1962) used the Modern Language Aptitude Test with a year-group of Scottish children about to start learning French. At the end of the first year, a test of French provided the criterion to measure the predictive value of the Aptitude Test. There was, as we said before, a reasonably close agreement between test and criterion. That is to say, the test was successful in identifying in advance those who would have difficulty in learning French. What then is the implication? Are we to exclude pupils who score low in the test from the French course, to save them from failure and avoid a waste of the teacher's effort? Or do we ignore the test, even if there is a shortage of good teachers and there are other subjects where the prognosis for learning is much more hopeful? Or has the test merely shown that these pupils will not learn French by the method which has been used, and therefore a different approach should be tried for them?

Research seldom gives a simple answer to a question. Rather, it focuses our thinking, narrowing down the questions and indicating the basis on which a decision should be made. This is the way in which results must be interpreted, not as putting an end to inquiry, but stimulating it and giving it precision.

SUMMARY

The interpretation of the results of educational research requires considerable skill and experience. Certain recurring dangers can be identified. The *post hoc ergo propter hoc* fallacy warns against formulating hypotheses in retrospect and applying these to data already collected. A repeat study must be used instead. The same fallacy is also present in the temptation to assume a causal relation between variables, and also to interpret a direction. Does intelligence cause attainment or can the effect also work, to some extent, in the other direction as well?

False interpretation of results can also follow the use of an inappropriate or inadequate criterion in prediction studies or in a study where a whole series of variables are being related to school attainment. The criterion must be the strongest measure, valid, reliable and meaningful in normal practical terms. Statistical artifacts also cause problems. Homogeneous samples cause attenuation of correlation coefficients. Regression to the mean will occur if extreme groups are used, while multiple regression techniques over-emphasize chance variations in relations. Cross-validation—the replication of a study to make sure that the result was no fluke—is important in much educational research, but not often to be found.

| Writing the Report

Writing the report of a research project always takes longer than one hopes. Often it seems a tedious chore. Yet if the results are not communicated effectively, they will be overlooked. Effective communication is the researcher's responsibility and no one else's: he alone is to blame if no one can understand what he has done or judge its value appropriately. Chapter 2 listed the three parts of a project, which deserve approximately equal shares of the time available: the planning, the work itself and the writing up. But the writing should not all be left to the end. Much of the burden can be removed if the work is written up as the investigation proceeds. By the end of the planning stage, the opening sections of the report should be already in first draft, and the description of relevant previous work may be virtually complete. Few research workers do what they ought to do and keep systematic records of work done on a uniform size of paper for convenient reference; but all subsequently regret the deplorable tendency to make notes on the back of envelopes and on scraps of paper, which is such a handicap when the report comes to be written.

## RESEARCH REPORTS

The aim of a research report is to convey information in a form which is readily accessible to other scholars. Consequently, there is a conventional form of reporting an experimental investigation. Not every report fits this pattern exactly, but unnecessary departures from it are an obstacle to communication. Originality finds expression in the ideas, not in the form of report. The framework is:

1. An outline of the research.
2. A review of previous work.
3. A precise statement of the scope and aims of the investigation.
4. Description of the procedure, the sample and the tests or measurements used.
5. Statement of results.
6. Discussion.
7. Summary and conclusions.
8. List of references.

The general style of the report is impersonal, but this does not mean that it must all be in the passive voice. It does mean excluding the word 'I', and, even more important, such phrases as 'in my opinion'. 'In the opinion of the writer' is no better. The reader is interested in your evidence and not your opinion. Clarity, simplicity of style and brevity are the cardinal virtues. As with other virtues, they are sometimes incompatible: a phrase like 'verbal reasoning test score' may have to be repeated even if 'intelligence' is both simple and brief. Abbreviations are inexcusable except for the most widely known, like 'GCE', and even these should be given in full on the first occasion they occur, since the report may be read by someone who is unfamiliar with them. Technical terms should be avoided in sections 1, 3 and 7 in the framework listed above. In the other sections the use of technical terms may be inevitable, but not jargon, in the sense of unnecessary technical language which can be expressed simply.

Section 1, the outline of research, is a fairly brief general statement of the background to the problem, to give the setting of the investigation and point out its importance. Section 2, the review of previous work, follows on from this. Ideally it should be a reasoned and readable sequence of arguments and evidence, leading into section 3 which sets out the specific purpose and scope of the investigation to be reported. The review of previous work should not be just a series of abstracts of papers: the studies quoted should be grouped to bring out the main themes or principles in the work reviewed. References are conventionally given by adding the date in brackets after the author's name, or by giving author and date in brackets. This is easier than the use of footnotes, which add to the typist's problems.

Section 3, the statement of the scope and aims of the investigation, should be straightforward and brief. Details and arguments are out of place here: the intention is to enable a reader to find out precisely what the inquiry involved. By contrast, section 4 contains the details of procedure, the full description of the sample, and information about the tests or measurements used. Standard tests and procedures which are generally well known need not be described; but when ratings or teachers' estimates have been used, a full account of how these were obtained is necessary to allow the reader to judge their value. A scale or technique specially devised for the investigation should be described in full in an appendix at the end.

The structure of section 5, the statement of results, is determined by the tables in which results are presented. Each table is numbered and has a title which is intelligible without reference to the text. The text itself in this section is little more than a linking commentary to the tables. Inferences from the results should not be included here: this is a factual section about which there should be no dispute. The commentary may appropriately call attention to aspects of the results which are to be discussed in the next section.

Section 6 is the discussion of results, in which interpretations and judgements are made. A special effort should be made to keep this section under control, and to limit the conclusions to what can reasonably be justified by the evidence. These conclusions are brought together in a brief section 7. This section is sometimes written as a summary of the investigation, listing in three short paragraphs the aim, scope and findings.

The list of references should be set out alphabetically by author's name. Only titles referred to in the text should be included here: the list is not intended as a bibliography on the subject. To a reader who is himself planning research in this field, this may be the most important part of the report. Again, there is a conventional form for references which must be observed: examples are to be found in the references at the end of this book. A journal article is described by author, initials, date, title of article, title of journal, volume number, page numbers. A book is described by author, initials, date, title, place of publication, publisher. Details of accepted abbreviations and other conventions are given in the British Psychological Society's pamphlet, *Suggestions to Authors* (BPS, 18–19 Albemarle Street, London WIX LDN, 1967).

An additional section which has not so far been mentioned is a simple statement of acknowledgement to those who have assisted in the investigation. This is often inserted at the beginning of a report, immediately after the list of contents. Expecially when teachers and headmasters have helped with an investigation, a personal expression of thanks—and, perhaps more important, a brief summary of results sent to each personally—is a necessary recognition of the extent to which research is dependent on their help and tolerance. (Further guidance on procedure is given in the appendix, p. 177.)

This description of the structure of a research report has touched on only a few important points. The student who is writing a report for the first time—and others, too, who consider themselves experienced—would be well advised to consult Wiseman's short booklet, *Reporting Research in Education* (1952). This can be read in less than one hour, but will save many hours of labour in writing. Guiding principles, specific examples and useful suggestions are set out simply and lucidly. The pamphlet itself is a model of the style it recommends.

Why should this pattern of reporting be prescribed so rigidly? The answer will be found in the first paragraph of this chapter. The purpose of a research report is to communicate results, and the volume of research publications is now so overwhelming that no active research worker has time to read reports through from cover to cover. He must be selective, reading certain sections at very high speed because they deal with familiar previous research or give details to which he will refer back only if he wishes to check some finding. A research report is not a story: it is an arrangement of information. Because the information is laid out in a standard form, a reader can discover quickly what he wants to know about a piece of research.

Few readers start at the beginning of a research report and read through to the end. Similarly, the way to write a report is not necessarily to start with chapter 1. Each person must find the pattern of writing which suits him best. But often, section 2, the review of previous work can be written first; and section 4, the details of procedure, sample and measurements, can be sketched out at an early stage. Section 3, the precise statement of the scope and aims of the inquiry is so brief that it can be put into its final form at a late stage; but a first draft must be prepared at a very early stage in planning. Writing down in a single page an outline of what is planned is a valuable way to test the adequacy of a plan, and a provisional outline like this is a useful touchstone at a later stage in deciding the relevance of this or that aspect.

The heart of a report is section 5, the statement of results. When the analysis of data is complete, and the research worker turns to face the task of writing, his first step should be to design the lay-out of the tables in section 5. This requires careful thought and frequent revision, to obtain a proper balance between detail and conciseness, and to develop a logical sequence of presentation. Once the tables are ready, the rest of section 5 is easy.

The Discussion section is possibly the hardest section to write, because it is difficult to know how much to include. Most discussions are too long, and too long-winded. Readers appreciate quality and are wearied by quantity. This is the one sure guide in writing this section.

With Results and Discussion complete, Previous Work more or less in final draft, section 4 fairly well sketched out, and a provisional version of the Statement of Research for section 3, sections 1 and 7, the General Outline and the Summary and Conclusions can now be tackled. Section 8, the List of References, should not be left to the end. Inevitably, it turns out that some detail has not been noted—an author's initial, a volume number, a date of publication. Checking the references and filling gaps takes time, but it will be done methodically by the research worker who has experienced the frustration of an incomplete or incorrect reference in some other writer's work.


## RESEARCH PAPERS

The previous section deals with the writing of a thesis or a report which is to be circulated in typescript. A report for presentation at a scientific meeting requires a different style altogether. The first rule is to find out how long the paper should be, subtract five minutes for unexpected delays in starting, and decide how much can be expressed in the remainder. A normal rate for public speaking is 120 words per minute, half the speed of conversational speech. The first five minutes will be required to allow the audience to 'tune in'. The scope and purpose—what and why —must be explained in a manner which will arouse interest. A writer who feels obliged to open with a conventional introduction of vague generalities should write it and then start at the second paragraph.

The main part of the paper should be grouped under a few headings, which should be stated clearly and repeated in presentation, so that the material has shape and its sequence and over-all pattern can be grasped. 'Sign-posting' phrases help: 'Two points should be stressed. . . .' 'Let me give you an example. . . .' 'The conclusion from this is. . . .' 'There is, of course, another way of explaining these results. . . .' A series of slides (usually not more than six), a blackboard outline (if it is short), or large and carefully prepared diagrams may be used to structure the presentation. Figures should always be written on a blackboard if few, on a hand-out if detailed. Other details, such as references or dates, must be presented with an orienting phrase: 'some ten years ago, in 1960. . . .'

The inexperienced speaker is well advised to read from a prepared script which he has rehearsed so that he can look at his audience most of the time. He must time the talk carefully in rehearsal. The capital sin is to over-run one's time: no scientific audience has ever complained that a paper is too short. Marking a section which can be omitted if time is short is a wise precaution.

The essential point is to realize that a paper read cannot include the detail of a printed paper, and this is not its function. Its function is to summarize and select, and to interest the audience in following up the points, possibly by reading the paper when it is published.

## PUBLISHED ARTICLES

Writing a paper for publication in a journal requires yet another style of presentation. The main considerations here are that publication may cost £10 per page, that tables take up space, that diagrams are costly, and a short paper is more likely to be published—and to be read—than a long one. The first three sections mentioned earlier, the general outline, the review of previous work and the precise description of the investigation, must be presented concisely. The details of the procedure, sampling and measurement techniques require fuller treatment. But results should be confined to significant findings: details of non-significant results are inappropriate. So are sentences such as: 'Owing to pressure of space, it is not practicable to review fully the detailed implications of the interactions of the many different variables: this paper is therefore limited to a consideration of the more important findings which emerged from analysis of the relevant data'. The editor will merely delete the lot.

Tables in particular should be scrutinized to check that they are really necessary. Simple data can often be more concisely reported in the text. Results should not be presented both in tables and diagrams. Advice on the preparation of a manuscript for publication is given in the pamphlet, *Suggestions to Authors*, which was mentioned earlier. The information given (especially on pp. 3–6) is particularly helpful because it sets out precisely the recommentations for articles submitted to the British Psychological Society's journals, and these apply also to other journals. For example, all copy (including references and footnotes) should be typed in double spacing, with wide margins, on substantial paper, not on flimsy nor in the form of carbon copies or duplicated prints. Many small details of presentation are covered, including the appropriate length of a title, the position and length of an 'Acknowledgements' section and how to indicate in the text the position where tables and diagrams (typed or drawn separately) are to appear. Procedure in handling proofs is outlined: these must be returned promptly, and new material cannot be written into an article once it has reached the proof stage.

Most authors think that editors and publishers are much too meticulous in prescribing these conditions in such detail. Nevertheless authors expect their papers to be printed correctly; and readers expect the articles in a journal to follow a standard pattern, to make it easy for them to read and refer to articles. Consequently, editors would name three particularly deadly sins among the many committed by contributors: breaking house rules; disorganization; and dodging.

'House rules' are the conventions which a journal applies in lay-out, terminology, references, footnotes, etc. If a writer has not examined a previous copy of the journal and observed its practice, an editor may be faced with the task of revising a whole page of references, and even with the recasting of a substantial part of an article. If there is any doubt about a paper, this will tip the balance against it. Usually the summary (often put at the beginning of a paper) is too long, if the author has remembered to include it at all. A three-sentence summary, stating the topic, the procedure and the results, is often sufficient.

The 'disorganized' writer uses the grapeshot technique. He throws in all his data, and writes a covering letter to the editor: 'If you think any changes are necessary, please do not hesitate to suggest these'. (Translation: 'Tell me what to do to get this published'.) Most papers try to cover too much. The author does not know what he wants to say and he leaves it to the reader to discover what his purpose is. Or worse, he leaves it to the editor. He should select one point as the main focus of his paper, and write the report around that point.

'Dodging' is a fine art, which editors know perhaps better than the authors who try it.

'The results obtained from three of the subjects were selected for detailed study.' (Translation: 'The results of the others didn't make sense and were therefore ignored'.)

'Previous research has shown that . . .' ('I couldn't be bothered to look up the references.')

'Results indicate that. . . .' ('I can't prove it, but this is what I believe.')

'Results suggest that . . . .' ('The results were not significant.')

'It is obvious that, well known that, generally accepted that. . . .' ('No evidence available.')

'This aspect requires further research.' ('I can't make head nor tail of it myself.')

'. . . . a pilot study . . . .' ('No significant results, but my promotion is coming up shortly.')

'A content analysis of forty-three items in the inventory identified eight distinguishable categories.' ('I looked at the cards and put them into eight piles.')

'Full details of the statistical procedure will be found in Guilford's *Psychometric Methods*.' ('I couldn't understand it myself.')

'A representative sample of university students.' ('My tutorial group.')

'Because of various complicating factors this group was omitted from the analysis.' ('I couldn't sort out the mess and scrapped the lot.')

Readers are invited to add to the collection from their study of the journals, or possibly from their own reports.

SUMMARY

Educational research, as described in this book, is a form of systematic inquiry which progresses through a series of well-defined stages. It should demonstrate the logical structure and hard reasoning to be found in the best scientific research, though the difficulty in measurement precludes the same precision in the results. The findings are rarely definitive and thus require careful interpretation.

The research report should reflect the whole research process. Logical structure and hard reasoning together with clarity, simplicity of style and brevity are cardinal virtues. The aim is to communicate the result effectively; any unnecessary details or clumsy wording distracts from this purpose. The structure of the research report reflects the stages in planning a research study, which were outlined in chapter 2. This scheme of presentation, though formal and artificial, does facilitate communication. It allows readers to anticipate where to search for the particular details they require, where to find a summary or a definition of the sample, for example.

Research in isolation serves no purpose. Effective communication, both to other research workers and to teachers and other educationists, is the essence of good educational research.

# Appendix

*Procedure for Research in Schools*

The Educational Research Board of the Social Science Research Council has prepared a pamphlet of advice for research workers and students on educational research in schools. By permission of the Board, the pamphlet is reproduced in this appendix, with an additional note on procedure in Scotland. Copies of the pamphlet may be obtained from SSRC on request.

## EDUCATIONAL RESEARCH IN SCHOOLS

### 1. *Introduction*

The Social Science Research Council through its Educational Research Board is awarding an increasing number of research grants in the field of education. It is naturally concerned to see that this research is carried out, not only competently, but with due consideration for the attitudes and interests of other people. Co-operation in research often depends on the establishment of good relations. The reputation of research is often at stake and a lapse of 'etiquette' can damage good relations both for the present and the future.

### 2. *Arranging your inquiry*

The main thing to remember is that schools are meant primarily for educating children, not for fostering research, and access to a school and its facilities is asked for as a favour , not demanded as a right. The usual, and often the required procedure, is to ask your supervisor to approach the local education authority, in the first instance, rather than the school itself unless you are already on the staff. Remember that some schools may have suffered a surfeit of research workers and naturally their heads may be more cautious in granting access to the classroom. It sometimes takes as much as *one complete term* to obtain permission for a school to be approached and then the final decision always rests with the head. The initial application for research facilities should always be accompanied by at least two copies of the relevant testing material and any plans affecting normal school routine. The head should also have a chance to see a project demonstrated if it is experimental.

### 3. *General considerations*

It is essential to report to the head as soon as you arrive.

Inquiries dealing with the staff, their qualifications, attitudes and methods should be avoided, unless they are germane to your inquiry, in which case prior consultation with teachers' associations is clearly desirable.

You should also realize that parents may raise strong objections if you ask their children highly personal questions about their feelings or about their homes. You should not take photographs of staff and children without seeking prior permission.

Remember that research is all too often strange to teachers, if not positively suspect, so please be tactful about this. At the same time, opportunities are likely to occur for interesting staff and pupils in research and even helping them to take an active part in it themselves.

### 4. *In the classroom*

After you have been introduced to a class, try to put the children at their ease and to engage their interest. They will probably regard a test as something out of the ordinary, while the test depends for its success upon their being in an ordinary frame of mind. It pays to reassure the children that it isn't an examination; their responses will be treated confidentially and not affect their school report or progress. It also pays to have prepared a clear brief statement of your aims, the methods you intend to use, and what the children will be asked to do. (This kind of statement also comes in handy in approaching the head in the first place and preparing a report on your research.)

The amount of time available in the classroom is not unlimited and careful pre-planning is required in order to complete your work programme without disruption of the school timetable. Below are a number of points which are worth checking on beforehand and which may save time (and embarrassment) in the classroom:

Check that your equipment is in good working order and that such spares as projector bulbs, fuses, batteries are at hand. Try to ensure that your plugs are compatible with the sockets at the school.

Check that your test material is complete.

Have various test papers in sets, ready to be handed to pupils. Have you previously informed the school that you will be using equipment? Some classrooms may not have the facilities for the use of equipment and the school routine could easily be disrupted at the last moment.

Has your timetable taken account of school assemblies and intervals?

Have you allowed sufficient time for handing out papers, explaining your objectives and answering pupils' questions?

## 5. *Preparation of your report*

It is not likely that an education authority will allow you to carry out an investigation within one of its schools unless it retains the right to see the report prior to publication. If your report contains any remarks that might be considered as critical of a school, its staff or pupils, you should neither mention it by the name or offer any other means of identification. Otherwise, you should acknowledge the assistance given to you by any heads, education officers, etc., in the preface to your report. It would help future good relations if the head were sent a copy of your report, if published. Perhaps the final point to remember is that a letter to the school, thanking the head, staff and pupils would be appreciated.

*Note on procedure in Scotland*

In Scotland, an agreed procedure has been established for the approval of requests for research facilities. The headmaster of any school has final authority in deciding whether or not a research project may be conducted within his school. Where a project involves one school only, or schools in a single education authority, the permission of the Director of Education is also required. He should be informed of the scope and purpose of the research, and be given details of the procedures involved, so that he can answer inquiries from parents or from Education Committee members. A project which involves pupils in more than one education authority must be referred to the Association of Directors of Education in Scotland, whose approval is necessary. In general, research is approved only when it is clear that it has educational relevance, is not time wasting for the pupils concerned and is planned or supervised by someone experienced in educational research. Approval is given on the understanding that it is open to any authority, school or teacher to withhold permission.

# References

ADAMS, J. (1922) *Modern Developments in Educational Practice*. London: University of London Press Ltd.

ALLPORT, G. W. (1961) *Pattern and Growth in Personality*. New York: Holt, Rinehart and Winston. (1st ed. 1937.)

ANASTASI, A. (1961) *Psychological Testing*. New York: Macmillan. (1st ed. 1954.)

ANSTEY, E. (1966) *Psychological Tests*. London: Nelson.

BALES, R. F. (1950) *Interaction Process Analysis: a Method for the Study of Small Groups*. Cambridge, Mass.: Addison-Wesley.

BENNETT, G. K., SEASHORE, H. G. and WESMAN, A. G. (1966) *Differential Aptitude Tests*. New York: Psychological Corporation. (1st ed. 1947).

BERNSTEIN, B. (1961) 'Social class and linguistic development: a theory of social learning.' See Halsey *et al.* (1961).

BLOOM, B. S. (ed.) (1956) *Taxonomy of Educational Objectives: Handbook I, The Cognitive Domain*. London: Longmans.

BORG, W. R. (1963) *Educational Research: an Introduction*. London: Longmans.

British Psychological Society (1967) *Suggestions to Authors*. London: British Psychological Society.

BUROS, O. K. (ed.) (1965) *The Sixth Mental Measurements Yearbook*. New York: Gryphon Press.

BUROS, O. K. (1965) *Tests in Print*. New York: Gryphon Press.

BURSTALL, C. (1968) *French from Eight: a National Experiment*. London: NFER.

BURT, C. (1922) *Mental and Scholastic Tests*. London: Staples.

BURT, C. (1937) *The Backward Child*. London: University of London Press Ltd.

BUTCHER, H. J. (1966) *Sampling in Educational Research*. Manchester: Manchester University Press.

BUTCHER, H. J. (1968) *Human Intelligence*. London: Methuen.

BUXTON, C. E. (1966) 'Evaluations of forced-choice and Likert-type tests of motivation to academic achievement.' *Br. J. educ. Psychol.*, **36**, 192–201.

CARROLL, J. B. and SAPON, S. M. (1955) *Modern Language Aptitude Test.* New York: Psychological Corporation.

CATTELL, R. B. (1956, 1963) *16-PF. High School Personality Questionnaire (HSPQ). Children's Personality Questionnaire (CPQ).* Champaign: Institute for Personality and Ability Testing.

CATTELL, R. B. (1965) *The Scientific Analysis of Personality.* Harmondsworth, Middlesex: Penguin.

CONNAUGHTON, I. M. and SKURNIK, L. S. (1969) 'The comparative effectiveness of several short-cut item-analysis procedures.' *Br. J. educ. Psychol.*, **39**, 230–4.

COOK, W. W., LEEDS, C. H. and CALLIS, R. (1951) *Minnesota Teacher Attitude Inventory.* New York: Psychological Corporation.

CRONBACH, L. J. (1964a) *Essentials of Psychological Testing.* New York: Harper.

CRONBACH, L. J. (1964b) In ROSENBLOOM, P. C. (ed.) *Modern Viewpoints in the Curriculum.* New York: McGraw-Hill.

CSE Examination Bulletin No. 4 (1964) *An Introduction to Objective-type Examinations.* London: H.M. Stationery Office.

CSE Examination Bulletin No. 5 (1965) *School-based Examinations.* London: H.M. Stationery Office.

CSE Examination Bulletin No. 12 (1966) *Multiple Marking of English Compositions.* London: H.M. Stationery Office.

Department of Education and Science (1966) *Progress in Reading,* 1948–64. London: H.M. Stationery Office.

Department of Education and Science (1967) *Children and their Primary Schools* (The Plowden Report). 2 vols. London: H.M. Stationery Office.

DOLL, E. A. (1947) *Vineland Social Maturity Scale.* Minneapolis: Educational Test Bureau.

DONALDSON, M. (1963) *A Study of Children's Thinking.* London: Tavistock.

DOWNING, J. (1967) *The i.t.a. Symposium: Research Report on the British Experiment with i.t.a.* London: NFER.

Educational Testing Service (1964) *Short-Cut Statistics for Teacher-Made Tests.* Princeton: Educational Testing Service.

EDWARDS, A. L. (1957) *Techniques of Attitude Scale Construction.* New York: Appleton-Century.

EVANS, K. M. (1962) *Sociometry and Education*. London: Routledge & Kegan Paul.

FLEXNER, A. (1930) *Universities, American, English, German*. London: Oxford University Press.

FRASER, E. D. (1959) *Home Environment and the School*. London: University of London Press Ltd.

GAGNÉ, R. M. (1967) *Learning and Individual Differences*. Columbus, Ohio: Merrill.

GESELL, A., *et al.* (1940, 1946, 1956) *The First Five Years of Life. The Child from Five to Ten. Youth: The Years from Ten to Sixteen*. New York: Harper.

GLASS, D. V. (ed.) (1954) *Social Mobility in Britain*. London: Routledge & Kegan Paul.

GOLDMAN, R. J. (1964) 'The Minnesota Tests of Creative Thinking.' *Educ. Res.*, **7**, 3–14.

GUILFORD, J. P. (1950) 'Creativity.' *Am. Psychol.*, **5**, 444–54.

HALLWORTH, H. J. (1965) *A System of Computer Programs for Use in Psychology and Education*. London: British Psychological Society.

HALSEY, A. H., FLOUD, J. and ANDERSON, C. A. (1961) *Education, Economy and Society*. New York: Free Press of Glencoe.

HENRYSSON, S. (1964) 'Equalising school marks in Sweden.' *College Board Rev.*, **52**, 21–3.

HIRST, P. (1965) 'Liberal education and the nature of knowledge.' In ARCHAMBAULDT, R. D. (ed.) *Philosophical Analysis and Education*. London: Routledge & Kegan Paul.

HUDSON, L. (1966) *Contrary Imaginations*. London: Methuen.

HUDSON, L. (1968) *Frames of Mind*. London: Methuen.

JACKSON, L. (1952) *A Test of Family Attitudes*. London: Methuen.

JACKSON, S. (1969) *A Teacher's Guide to Tests and Testing*. London: Longmans (1st ed. 1968).

KERR, J. F. (ed.) (1968) *Changing the Curriculum*. London: University of London Press Ltd.

KIRKWOOD, M. (1962) 'The Carroll and Sapon Modern Language Aptitude Test.' M.Ed. thesis, University of Aberdeen.

KRATHWOHL, D. R., BLOOM, B. S. and MASIA, B. B. (1964) *Taxonomy of Educational Objectives: Handbook II, The Affective Domain*. London: Longmans.

LEITH, G. O. M. (1966) *A Handbook of Programmed Learning*. Birmingham: University of Birmingham Educational Review Occasional Bulletin No. 1. (1st ed. 1964.)

LEWIS, D. G. (1967) *Statistical Methods in Education*. London: University of London Press Ltd.

LEWIS, D. G. (1968) *Experimental Design in Education*. London: University of London Press Ltd.

London Association for the Teaching of English (1965) *Assessing Compositions*. London: Blackie.

LUNN, J. C. B. (1969) 'The development of scales to measure junior school children's attitudes.' *Br. J. educ. Psychol.*, **39**, 64–71.

LUNZER, E. (1966) *The Manchester Scales of Social Adaptation*. London: NFER.

MCINTOSH, D. M., WALKER, D. A. and MACKAY, D. (1962) *The Scaling of Teachers' Marks and Estimates*. Edinburgh: Oliver and Boyd. (1st ed. 1949.)

MCLEISH, J., KNIGHT, M. and DAVIS, T. (1968) *Lot's Wife: an Experiment in Sensitivity Training for Student Teachers*. Cambridge: University of Cambridge Institute of Education (cyclostyled).

MATTHEWS, G. (1964) Nuffield Mathematics Project, Bulletin No. 1. London: Nuffield Foundation.

Ministry of Aviation (1964) *Programming in ALGOL*. London: H.M. Stationery Office.

Ministry of Education (1954) *Early Leaving*. Report of the Central Advisory Council on Education (England). London: H.M. Stationery Office.

Ministry of Education (1963) *Half Our Future* (The Newsom Report). Report of the Central Advisory Council on Education (England). London: H. M. Stationery Office.

MOONEY, R. L. (1950) *Mooney Problem Check List*. New York: Psychological Corporation.

MORTON-WILLIAMS, R., FINCH, S. and POLL, C. (1966) *Undergraduates' Attitudes to Teaching as a Career*. Social Survey Report, 354.

MORTON-WILLIAMS, R. and FINCH, S. (1968) See Schools Council, 1968a.

MOSER, C. A. (1958) *Survey Methods in Social Investigation*. London: Heinemann.

MURRAY, H. A. (1943) *Thematic Apperception Test*. Cambridge, Mass.: Harvard University Press.

NEAGLEY, R. L. and EVANS, N. D. (1967) *Handbook of Effective Curriculum Development*. New Jersey: Prentice-Hall.

NISBET, J. D. (1953) *Family Environment*. London: Eugenics Society and Cassell.

NISBET, J. D. (1960) 'Frequency counts and their uses.' *Educ. Res.*, **3**, 51–64.

NISBET, J. D. and ENTWISTLE, N. J. (1969) *The Transition to Secondary Education*. London: University of London Press Ltd.

NUNNALLY, J. C. (1967) *Psychometric Theory*. New York: McGraw-Hill.

PERCIVAL, T. S. (1963) *A Standard French Grammar Test. A Standardised French Vocabulary Test*. London: University of London Press Ltd.

PIDGEON, D. and YATES, A. (1968) *An Introduction to Educational Measurement*. London: Routledge & Kegan Paul.

Registrar-General (1960) *Classification of Occupations, 1960*. General Register Office. London: H.M. Stationery Office.

RICE, J. M. (1897) 'The futility of the spelling grind.' *Forum*, 23.

ROBERTS, J. A. F. (1939) 'Intelligence and family size.' *Eugen. Rev.*, **30**, 237–47.

ROBERTSON, A. G. (1969) 'Mathematics.' In NISBET, J. (ed.) *Scottish Education Looks Ahead*. Edinburgh: Chambers.

RUDD, W. G. A. (1969) *Assessment of New Curricula through Field Trials*. Manchester: University of Manchester School of Education (cyclostyled).

SARASON, S. B., DAVIDSON, K. S., LIGHTALL, F. F., WAITE, R. R. and RUEBUSH, B. K. (1960) *Anxiety in Elementary School Children*. New York: Wiley.

SCHONELL, F. J. (1942) *Backwardness in the Basic Subjects*. Edinburgh: Oliver and Boyd.

Schools Council (1967*a*) *Curriculum Development: Teachers' Groups and Centres*. Working Paper No. 10. London: H. M. Stationery Office.

Schools Council (1967*b*) *Society and the Young School Leaver*. Working Paper No. 11. London: H. M. Stationery Office.

Schools Council (1968*a*) *Enquiry 1: Young School Leavers*. London: H. M. Stationery Office.

Schools Council (1968*b*) *The First Three Years, 1964–7*. London: H.M. Stationery Office.

Scottish Council for Research in Education (1949) *The Trend of Scottish Intelligence*. London: University of London Press Ltd.

Scottish Council for Research in Education (1953) *Social Implications of the 1947 Scottish Mental Survey*. London: University of London Press Ltd.

Scottish Education Department (1969) *Consultative Committee on the Curriculum: First Report 1965/8.* Edinburgh: H.M. Stationery Office.

STOTT, D. H. (1956) *Bristol Social Adjustment Guides.* London: University of London Press Ltd.

TAYLOR, C. W. (1964) *Creativity: Progress and Potential.* New York: McGraw-Hill.

TAYLOR, P. H. (1966) *Purpose and Structure in the Curriculum.* Inaugural lecture: University of Birmingham.

THURSTONE, L. L. (1947) *Vocational Interest Schedule.* New York: Psychological Corporation.

TORRANCE, E. P. (1962) *Guiding Creative Talent.* New York: Prentice-Hall.

TORRANCE, E. P. (1963) *Education and the Creative Potential.* Minneapolis: University of Minnesota Press.

VENESS, T. (1962) *School-Leavers: their Aspirations and Expectations.* London: Methuen.

VERNON, P. E. (1953) *Personality Tests and Assessments.* London: Methuen.

VERNON, P. E. (1955) 'The psychology of intelligence and "$g$".' *Bull. Br. psychol. Soc.,* **26**, 1–14.

VERNON, P. E. (ed.) (1957) *Secondary School Selection.* London: Methuen.

VERNON, P. E. (1960) *Intelligence and Attainment Tests.* London: University of London Press Ltd.

WALLACH, M. A. and KOGAN, N. (1965) *Modes of Thinking in Young Children.* New York: Holt, Rinehart and Winston.

WARBURTON, F. W. (1966) 'The construction of the new British Intelligence Scale.' *Bull. Br. psychol. Soc.,* **63**, 59.

WILLIAMS, J. H. (1916) 'The Whittier Scale for grading home conditions.' *J. Delinq.,* **I**, 271–86.

WISEMAN, S. (1949) 'The marking of English compositions in grammar school selection.' *Br. J. educ. Psychol.,* **19**, 200–9.

WISEMAN, S. (1952) *Reporting Research in Education.* Manchester: Manchester University Press.

WISEMAN, S. (1964) *Education and Environment.* Manchester: Manchester University Press.

YATES, A. and PIDGEON, D. (1957) *Admission to Grammar Schools.* London: Newnes.

# Acknowledgements

The authors wish to thank Professor H. J. Butcher and Mr D. E. Shanks for their helpful comments on a first draft, and Mrs May Boyd and Miss June Sallis, who typed successive versions of the text.

The authors and publishers would also like to thank the Controller of H.M. Stationery Office for permission to reprint excerpts from volume 2 of *Children and their Primary Schools* (the Plowden Report), International Computers Limited for permission to reprint figure 6, page 60, and Professor Liam Hudson, Methuen & Co. Ltd and Schocken Books Inc., New York, for permission to reprint excerpts from *Contrary Imaginations*.

# Index

ability,
  definition of, 76
  group tests of, 81
  individual tests of, 81
  measurement of, 76ff.
Adams, J., 144
*Admission to Grammar Schools*, 97
Allport, G. W., 114
analysis of variance, 14
Anastasi, A., 77
Anstey, E., 77, 79, 121
aptitude,
  definition of, 76
  tests of, 82
attainment,
  definition of, 76
  measurement of, 76ff.
  tests of, 83
attenuation, 162
attitude,
  definition of, 125
  measurement of, 125ff.
  pupils' self-ratings of, 121
attitude scales, 126ff.
  check lists, 132
  forced choice, 131
  Likert-type, 128
  paired comparisons, 131
  scalogram analysis, 130–31
  Thurstone-type, 127

*Backward Child, The*, 74
Bales, R. E., 137, 138
*Bender Gestalt Test*, 86
Bennett, G. K., Seashore, H. G. and
  Wesman, A. G., 82
Binet, A., 81, 107
Bloom, B. S., 148, 149
Borg, W. R., 51

*British Intelligence Scale*, 81
British Psychological Society, 170, 173
*British Social Adjustment Guides*, 132,
  140
Buros, O. K., 77
Burstall, C., 155
Burt, C., 74, 85
Butcher, H. J., 28, 76, 109
Buxton, C. E., 129, 131

Carroll, J. B. and Sapon, S. M., 83
case studies, 15, 140
Cattell, R. B., 114
causality, evidence of, 10, 157
Certificate of Secondary Education,
  84, 98, 100
*Changing the Curriculum*, 151
*Child from Five to Ten, The*, 140
*Children's Personality Questionnaire*, 114
*Classification of Occupations*, 68
coding,
  schedule, 58
  sheet, 58
  system for interviews, 40
computer programs, 63
Connaughton, I. M. and Skurnik,
  L. S., 90
Consultative Committee on the
  Curriculum, 154
*Contrary Imaginations*, 107
control group, 11
control of variables, 12
counselling and test profiles, 82
creativity, 106ff.
  definition of, 106
*Creativity: Progress and Potential*, 109
criterion, appropriate choice of, 161
Cronbach, L. J., 77, 151
cross-validation, 164

curriculum development, 144ff.
  aims and objectives, 147
  evaluation of, 151
  experimental method in, 154
  feedback of results, 153
  in Scotland, 153, 154
  stages in, 146
  systematic approach in, 144
Curriculum Study Group, 152

*Dalton Plan*, 144
data processing, 54ff.
  computer-input punched cards, 62
  hand-sorted cards, 58
  ledger method, 54
  machine-sorted cards, 61
  written cards, 55
demographic variables, 74
Department of Education and Science, 10, 153
dependent variable, 11
developmental tests, 86, 140
diagnostic tests, 84
*Differential Aptitude Test Battery*, 82
divergent thinking, 106ff.
Doll, E. A., 141
Donaldson, M., 86, 140
Downing, J., 80, 155–57

*Early Leaving*, 9, 65
*Education, Economy and Society*, 66
*Education and Environment*, 66, 74
*Educational Research*, 51
Edwards, A. L., 126, 129, 130
emotional instability, 114
environment, definition of, 65
environmental factors, 65ff.
*Essentials of Psychological Testing*, 77
Evans, K. M., 139
examination, essay-type, 101
examination marks, 92ff.
*Experimental Design in Education*, 14
experimental group, 11
experimental studies, 8ff.
extraversion, 114
Eysenck, H. J., 114, 117
*Eysenck Personality Inventory*, 117

face validity, 118
family size, 70
father's occupation, 65
*First Five Years of Life, The*, 140
*First Report*, 154
*First Three Years, The*, 153
Fisher, R. A., 26
Flexner, A., 53
*Frames of Mind*, 107
Fraser, E. D., 65, 71–75
*Frostig Developmental Test of Visual Perception*, 86

Gagné, R. M., 150
General Certificate of Education, 95, 104, 156, 160
Gesell, A., 140, 141
Glass, D. V., 70
Goldman, R. J., 106
Guilford, J. P., 106, 114

Hallworth, H. J., 63
Halo effect, 157
Halsey, A. H., Floud, J. and Anderson, C. A., 66
*Handbook of Programmed Learning*, 155
Hawthorne effect, 12, 156, 157
Henrysson, S., 95
Hirst, P., 147, 151
home, cultural and social level of, 71ff.
*Home Environment and the School*, 65
house, type of, 71
Hudson, L., 107, 109
*Human Intelligence*, 76

independent variable, 11
index,
  of discrimination, 88
  socio-economic, 72
*Intelligence and Attainment Tests*, 76
*Interaction Process Analysis*, 137
Interpretation, of research findings, 157ff.
interviews, 36ff.
  rapport in, 37, 41ff.
  standardised, 33
  unstructured, 42

interview schedule, pre-coding of, 40
*Introduction to Educational Measurement,*
    77
*Initial Teaching Alphabet,* 80, 155
*Initial Teaching Alphabet Symposium,*
    *The,* 157
item analysis, 88–90, 130

Jackson, L., 110
Jackson, S., 78
jingle fallacy, 118

Kerr, J. F., 148, 151
Kirkwood, M., 83, 165
Krathwohl, D. R., 148

Leith, G. O. M., 155
Lewis, D. G., 14, 57
Likert-type scales, 128–34
literature, review of, 17ff.
London Association for the Teaching
    of English, 100
Lunn, J. C. B., 131
Lunzer, E., 141

*Manchester Scales of Social Adaptation,*
    141
markers, differences between, 94
marking,
    schemes, 99
    use of reference scale, 100
marks,
    differences in ranges, 92
    difference in standard, 92
    scaling of, 95
    unscaled, 104
matched groups, 12
Mathematics Syllabus Committee, 154
Matthews, G., 146
McIntosh, D. M., Walker, D. A.
    and MacKay, D., 95
McLeish, J., 137
*Mental Measurements Yearbook,* 77,
    117
*Minnesota Teacher Attitude Inventory,*
    125
*Minnesota Tests of Creative Thinking,*
    107

*Modern Developments in Educational*
    *Practice,* 144
*Modern Language Aptitude Test,* 83, 165
*Modern Mathematics in Schools,* 154
*Modes of Thinking in Young*
    *Children,* 109
*Mooney Problem Check List,* 132
*Moray House Tests,* 82
Morton-Williams, R., Finch, S. and
    Poll, C., 39
Moser, C. A., 26
*Multiple Marking of English*
    *Compositions,* 100
multiple marking, of essays, 99
Murray, H. A., 110

National Foundation for Educational
    Research, 78, 82, 84, 131, 154–55
*National Survey of Parental Attitudes*
    *and Circumstances,* 36, 50
Neagley, R. L. and Evans, N. D., 147
*Newsom Report,* 148
Nisbet, J. D., 71, 154
Nisbet, J. D. and Entwistle, N. J.,
    112, 121
non-responders, to questionnaires, 52
Nuffield science and mathematics
    projects, 145–46
Nunnally, J. C., 77, 79

objectives, taxonomies of, 148
observation, systematic, 135ff.
over-achievers, 163

parents' education, 71
Percival, T. S., 84
performance tests, 81
personality,
    assessment of, 114ff.
    definition of, 114
    inventories, 116
    ratings by others, 119–20
    self-ratings, 115–16
*Personality Tests and Assessments,* 126
Peters, R. S., 147
Piaget, J., 86–87, 140
Pidgeon, D. and Yates, A., 77
planning research, stages of, 16ff.

*Plowden Report,* 10, 36, 49, 50, 66, 73–75, 161–62
population, definition of, 25
position in family, 70
*Programming in ALGOL,* 63
projective techniques, 110ff.
Psychological Corporation, The, 78
*Psychological Testing,* 77
*Psychological Tests,* 77
*Psychometric Theory,* 77

questionnaires, 44ff.
  lay-out, 48
  percentage response, 44
  wording questions, 47

randomisation of variables, 12
ranking procedures, 123
references, lay-out of, 169
*Registrar General's Scale,* 12, 30, 66, 68–69, 70, 75
Regression, 163
Reliability, 78, 90
*Reporting Research in Education,* 170
reports, writing-up research, 21, 167ff.
representative samples, 10, 25
research findings, educational implications of, 165
Rice, J. M., 9–11
Roberts, J. A. F., 71
Robertson, A. G., 154
Rudd, W. G. A., 152

sample,
  representative, 10, 25
  size of, 10, 25
*Sampling in Educational Research,* 28
sampling,
  frame, 27
  methods of, 24ff.
  ratio, 27
Sarason, S. B., 125
scaling examination marks, 95
*Scaling of Teachers' Marks and Estimates,* 95
scattergram, 57, 61
Schonell, F. J., 85–86, 99

*School-based Examinations,* 98
Schools Council, 144, 150, 153–54
Scotland,
  research procedure in, 179
  curriculum development in, 153–54
Scottish Certificate of Education, 104–5
Scottish Council for Research in Education, 10
Scottish Education Department, 154
*Scottish Mental Survey,* 10, 27
*Secondary School Selection,* 95
self-fulfilling prophecy, 162
sentence completion, 111
short-answer questions, 101
*Short-cut Statistics for Teacher-made Tests,* 103
social attitudes, 125
social class, 66ff.
*Social Implications of the 1947 Scottish Mental Survey,* 70
*Social Mobility in Britain,* 70
*Society and the Young School Leaver,* 150
sociometry, 139
*Sociometry and Education,* 139
sorting schedule, 57
statistical significance, 24
Stott, D. H., 132
*Suggestions to Authors,* 170, 173
*Survey Methods in Social Investigation,* 26
survey methods, 8ff.

Taylor, C. W., 109
Taylor, P. H., 147
*Teacher's Guide to Tests,* 78
*Techniques of Attitude Scale Construction,* 126
test construction, 87–90
*Tests in Print,* 78
*Test of Family Attitudes,* 110
tests,
  of ability, 81
  appropriate age range for, 79
  of aptitude, 82
  of attainment, 83
  closed, 82

tests—*continued*
  of creativity, 106
  cultural differences in, 80
  diagnostic, 84
  norms for, 78
  open, 82
  performance, 81
  standardised, 77ff.
Thurstone, L. L., 126, 131
*Thurstone-type scale*, 127, 128, 134
time sampling, 136
Torrance, E. P., 107, 109
*Transition to Secondary Education,*
  *The,* 112

under-achievers, 163
*Undergraduates' Attitudes to School*
  *Teaching as a Career,* 39
*Universities, American, English,*
  *German,* 53
*Universities Central Council on*
  *Admissions,* 104

validity, 78, 90
variables,
  dependent, 11
  independent, 11
variance, analysis of, 14
Veness, T., 112
Vernon, P. E., 76, 95, 125, 126
*Vineland Social Maturity Scale,* 141
*Vocational Interest Schedule,* 131

Wallach, M. A. and Kogan, N., 109
Warburton, F. W., 81
*Whittier Scale for Grading Home*
  *Conditions,* 72
Williams, J. H., 72
Wiseman, S., 66, 74, 99, 170
work cards, 150

Yates, A. and Pidgeon, D., 97
*Youth, The Years from Ten to Sixteen,*
  141

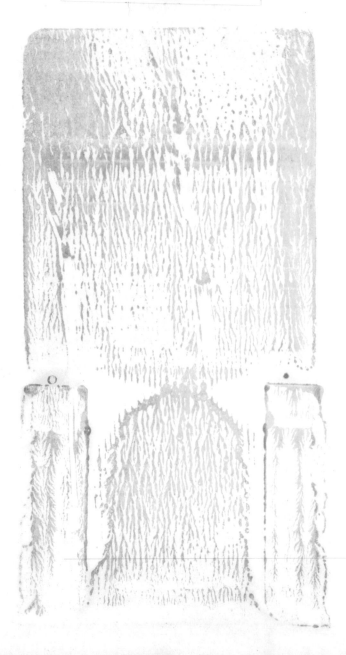